The Dutch
Coaching Notebook

The Ultimate Companion for Coaches of All Levels

by Henny Kormelink and Tjeu Seeverens

Published by
REEDSWAIN INC.

Library of Congress Cataloging - in - Publication Data

Kormelink, Henny and Seeverens, Tjeu
The Dutch Coaching Notebook/Henny Kormelink and Tjeu Seeverens

ISBN No. 0-9651020-9-2
Library of Congress Catalog Number - 97-68233
Copyright © 1997 Uitgeverij Eisma bv

This book was originally published in Dutch by Uitgeverij Eisma bv,
Post Office Box 340, 8901 BC Leeuwarden, The Netherlands.

Reedswain books are available at special discounts for bulk purchase. For
details, contact the Special Sales Manager at Reedswain.

REEDSWAIN, INC.
612 Pughtown Road • Spring City PA 19475
1-800-331-5191
Web Site: www.reedswain.com

Contents

Contents

 **Name**

Name

1	
2	
3	
4	
5	
6	
7	
8	
9	
10	
11	
12	
13	
14	
15	
16	
17	
18	

This Soccer Diary Belongs To:

Name_____

Address_____

City_____

State_____ Zip_____

Telephone_____

EMail:_____

Coach/Instructor of_____

Team

Training Sessions

Mon.	
Tues.	
Wed.	
Thurs.	
Fri.	
Sat.	
Sun.	

Soccer Addresses

Name_____

Address_____

Phone_____

Name_____

Address_____

Phone_____

Name_____

Address_____

Phone_____

Name_____

Address_____

Phone_____

Name_____

Address_____

Phone_____

Name_____

Address_____

Phone_____

Name_____

Address_____

Phone_____

Name_____

Address_____

Phone_____

Name_____

Address_____

Phone_____

Club Addresses

Name of Club: _____

Address: _____

City _____ State _____ Zip _____

Name	Addresses	Telephone
Committee:		
Youth Committee:		
Coaches:		

List of Players

Name	Date of Birth	Address

City	State/Zip Code	Telephone Number

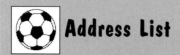

Address List

Name	Function

Address	Telephone

Overview Of Training Sessions & Matches

	January	February	March
1			
2			
3			
4			
5			
6			
7			
8			
9			
10			
11			
12			
13			
14			
15			
16			
17			
18			
19			
20			
21			
22			
23			
24			
25			
26			
27			
28			
29			
30			
31			

Overview Of Training Sessions & Matches

	April	May	June
1			
2			
3			
4			
5			
6			
7			
8			
9			
10			
11			
12			
13			
14			
15			
16			
17			
18			
19			
20			
21			
22			
23			
24			
25			
26			
27			
28			
29			
30			
31			

Overview Of Training Sessions & Matches

	July	August	September
1			
2			
3			
4			
5			
6			
7			
8			
9			
10			
11			
12			
13			
14			
15			
16			
17			
18			
19			
20			
21			
22			
23			
24			
25			
26			
27			
28			
29			
30			
31			

Overview Of Training Sessions & Matches

	October	November	December
1			
2			
3			
4			
5			
6			
7			
8			
9			
10			
11			
12			
13			
14			
15			
16			
17			
18			
19			
20			
21			
22			
23			
24			
25			
26			
27			
28			
29			
30			
31			

⚽ League Schedule

Date	Opponent	Score
		-
		-
		-
		-
		-
		-
		-
		-
		-
		-
		-
		-
		-
		-
		-
		-
		-
		-

League Schedule

Date	Opponent	Score
		-
		-
		-
		-
		-
		-
		-
		-
		-
		-
		-
		-
		-
		-
		-
		-
		-
		-

League Schedule

Date	Opponent	Score
		-
		-
		-
		-
		-
		-
		-
		-
		-
		-
		-
		-
		-
		-
		-
		-
		-
		-

League Schedule

Date	Opponent	Score
		-
		-
		-
		-
		-
		-
		-
		-
		-
		-
		-
		-
		-
		-
		-
		-
		-
		-

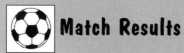

Match Results

No.	Date	L C F	H A	Opponent	Score	Half-time Score
1						
2						
3						
4						
5						
6						
7						
8						
9						
10						
11						
12						
13						
14						
15						
16						
17						
18						

L = League   H = Home   C = Cup   A = Away   F = Friendly

No.	Date	L C F	H A	Opponent	Score	Half-time Score
19						
20						
21						
22						
23						
24						
25						
26						
27						
28						
29						
30						
31						
32						
33						
34						
35						
36						

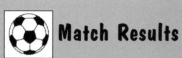

Match Results

No.	Date	L C F	H A	Opponent	Score	Half-time Score
37						
38						
39						
40						
41						
42						
43						
44						
45						
46						
47						
48						
49						
50						
51						
52						
53						
54						

L = League   H = Home   C = Cup   A = Away   F = Friendly

No.	Date	L C F	H A	Opponent	Score	Half-time Score
55						
56						
57						
58						
59						
60						
61						
62						
63						
64						
65						
66						
67						
68						
69						
70						
71						
72						

Match Results

	●						
		●					
			●				
				●			
					●		
						●	
							●

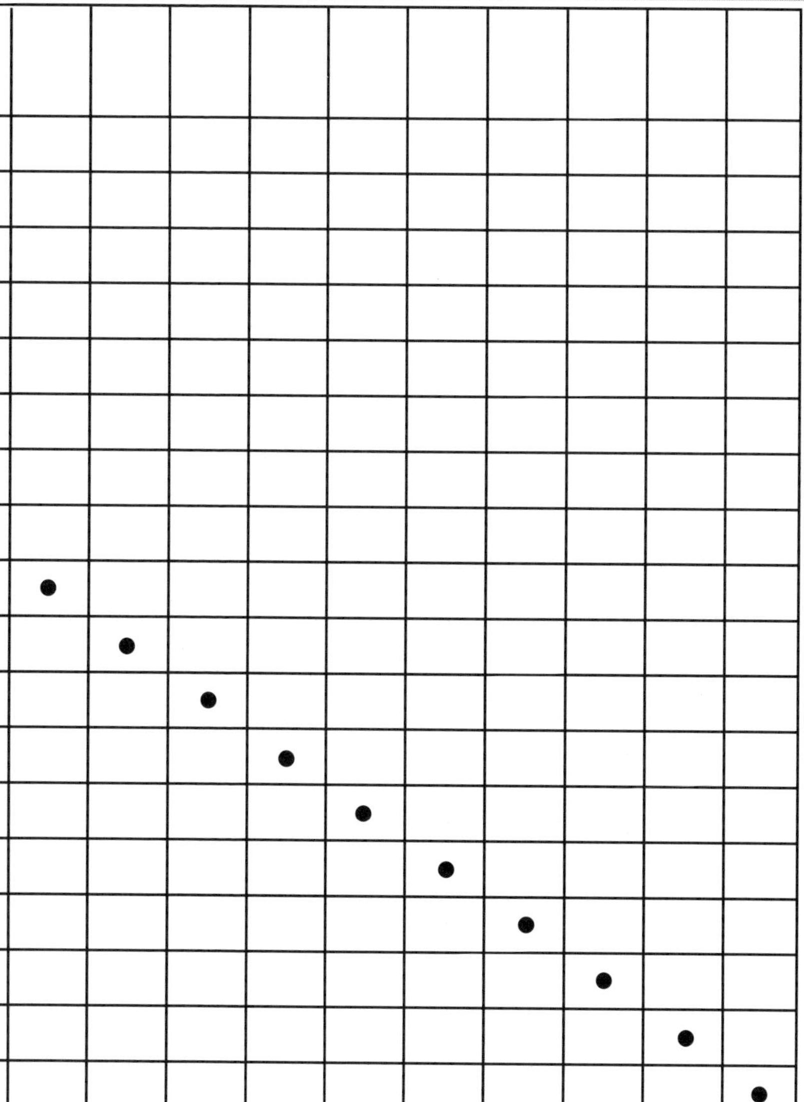

League Position Game by Game

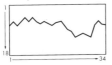

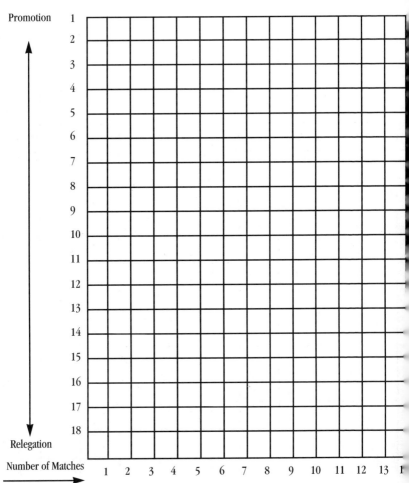

Promotion

	1
	2
	3
	4
	5
	6
	7
	8
	9
	10
	11
	12
	13
	14
	15
	16
	17
	18

Relegation

Number of Matches   1   2   3   4   5   6   7   8   9   10   11   12   13   1

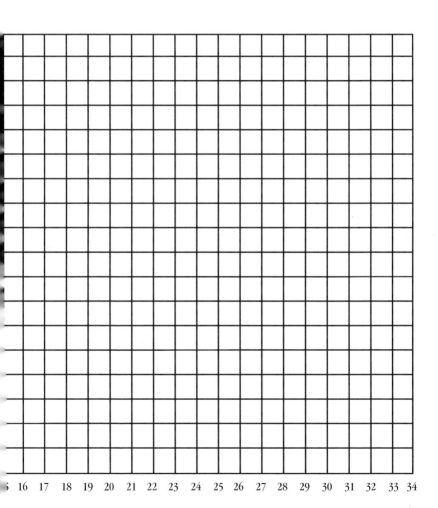

League Points Game by Game

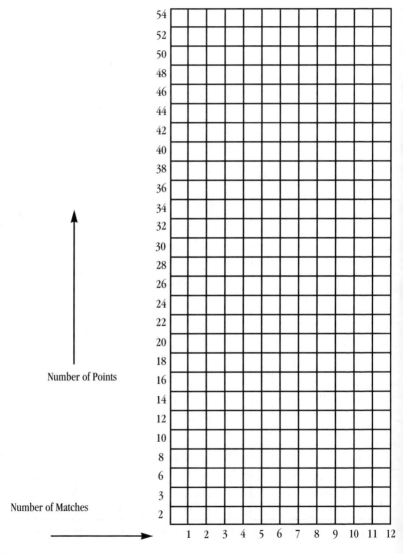

Number of Points

Number of Matches

27

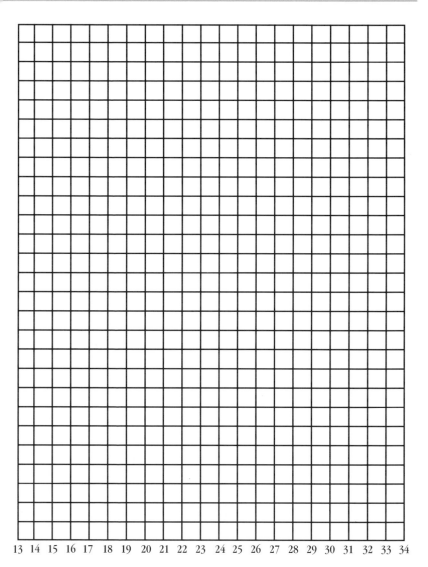

13 14 15 16 17 18 19 20 21 22 23 24 25 26 27 28 29 30 31 32 33 34

Players Used

Name	1	2	3	4	5	6	7

8	9	10	11	12	13	14	15	16	17	18	19	20

Players Used

Name	21	22	23	24	25	26	27

28	29	30	31	32	33	34	35	36	37	38	39	40

Top Scorers List (League Games) Goals per

Matches →												
Name	1	2	3	4	5	6	7	8	9	10	11	12

13	14	15	16	17	18	19	20	21	22	23	24	25	26	27	28	29	30	Total

Injuries

Name	Type

Notes

Comments

Injuries

Name	Type

Notes

Comments

Suspensions

Month														
Day														
Date														
Name														

Attendance at Training Sessions

Month														
Day														
Date														
Name														

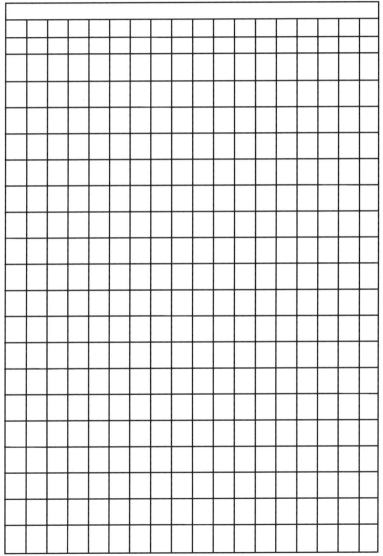

Attendance at Training Sessions

Month														
Day														
Date														
Name														

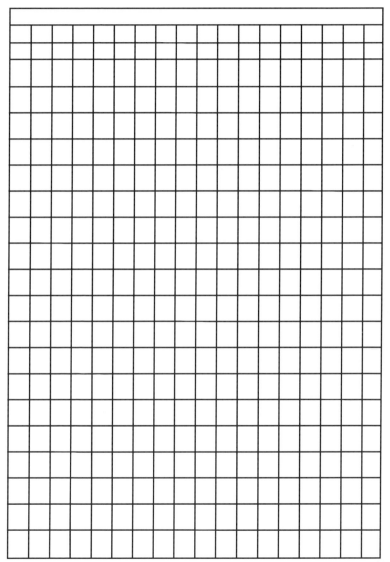

Attendance at Training Sessions

Month														
Day														
Date														
Name														

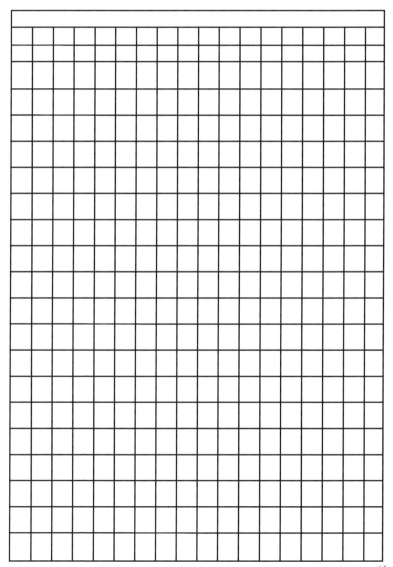

Coaching Program

	Month											
	Day											
	Date											
Passing Techniques												
Controlling the Ball												
Feinting												
Dribbling												
Basic Techniques												
Beating an Opponent 1 v 1												
Shooting												
Heading												
Exercises to Develop • Strength												
Speed												
Endurance												
Suppleness												
Dexterity												
Small Sided Games												
Combination Play												
1-2 Combinations												
3 v 1/ 3 v 2												
4 v 2 / 4 v 3												
2 v 2 / 3 v 3 / 4 v 4												
5 v 5 / 6 v 6 / 7 v 7												
1 v 2 / 2 v 3 / 3 v 4												
Attack v Defense												
11 v 11												
Corner												
Free Kick												
Goalkeeper Coaching												

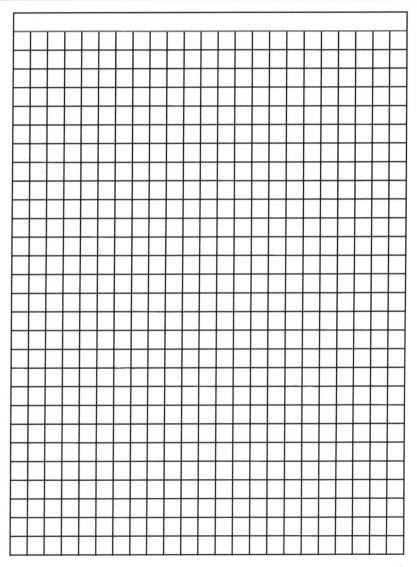

Coaching Program

	Month											
	Day											
	Date											
Passing Techniques												
Controlling the Ball												
Feinting												
Dribbling												
Basic Techiques												
Beating an Opponent 1 v 1												
Shooting												
Heading												
Exercises to Develop • Strength												
Speed												
Endurance												
Suppleness												
Dexterity												
Small Sided Games												
Combination Play												
1-2 Combinations												
3 v 1/ 3 v 2												
4 v 2 / 4 v 3												
2 v 2 / 3 v 3 / 4 v 4												
5 v 5 / 6 v 6 / 7 v 7												
1 v 2 / 2 v 3 / 3 v 4												
Attack v Defense												
11 v 11												
Corner												
Free Kick												
Goalkeeper Coaching												

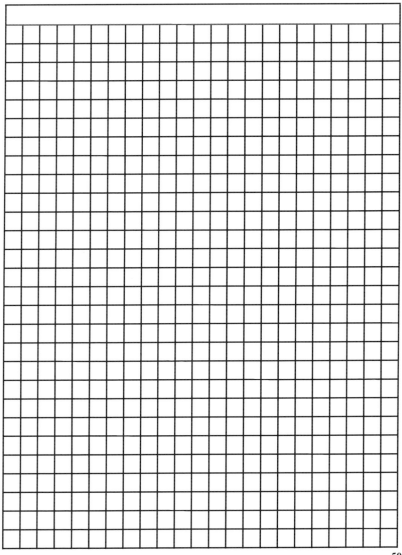

Test Scores   Date:

Name \ Skill	Dribbling	Passing	Shooting	Trapping	1 v 1	Heading	Speed	Endurance	Total

Name \ Skill	Dribbling	Passing	Shooting	Trapping	1 v 1	Heading	Speed	Endurance	Total

⚽ Test Scores   Date:

Name \ Skill	Dribbling	Passing	Shooting	Trapping	1 v 1	Heading	Speed	Endurance	Total

Name \ Skill	Dribbling	Passing	Shooting	Trapping	1 v 1	Heading	Speed	Endurance	Total

Restart Plays

Corner Attacking

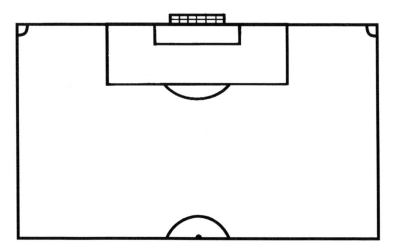

Corner Attacking

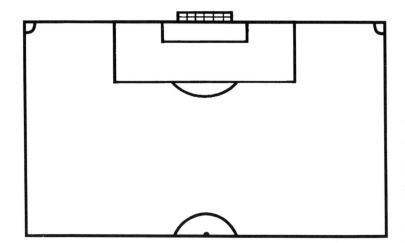

Restart Plays

Corner Defending

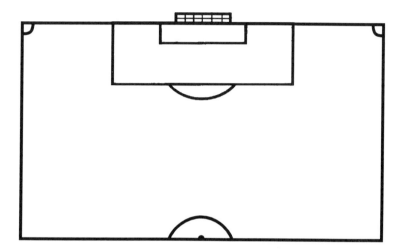

Corner Defending

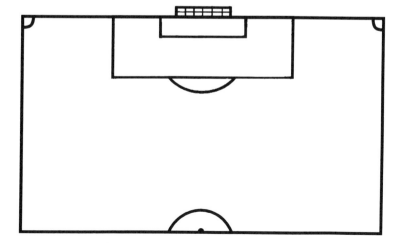

Restart Plays

Free Kick Defending

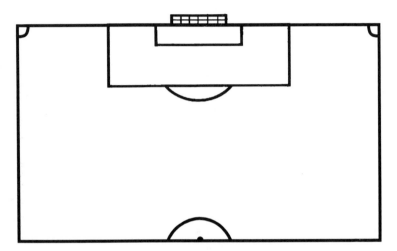

Free Kick Defending

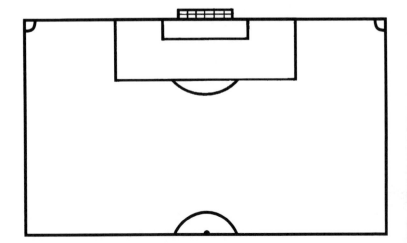

Restart Plays

Free Kick Attacking

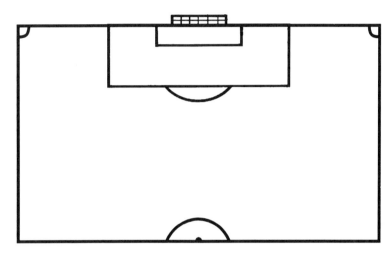

Free Kick Attacking

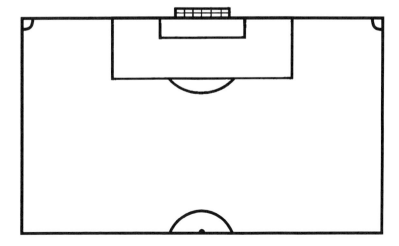

58

Match

Date_____

Date		Score
	_____vs_____	

Match

Date_____

Date		Score
	_____vs_____	

 **Match**   **Date**_____

Date		Score
	_____vs_____	

Match   **Date**_____

Date		Score
	_____vs_____	

Notes

 **Match**   **Date**_____

Date		Score
	_____vs_____	

 **Match**   **Date**_____

Date		Score
	_____vs_____	

Match

Date_____

Date		Score
	_____vs_____	

71

Date		Score
	_____vs_____	

 **Match**   **Date**_____

Date		Score
	_____vs_____	

Notes

Match   **Date**_____

Date		Score
	_____vs_____	

Match

Date_____

Date		Score
	_____vs_____	

Notes

80

 **Match**

Date_____

Date		Score
	_____vs_____	

Match   **Date**_____

Date		Score
	_____vs_____	

Match   **Date**_____

Date		Score
	_____vs_____	

Match

Date_____

Date		Score
	_____VS_____	

87

Match

Date_____

Date		Score
	_____vs_____	

Date		Score
	_____vs_____	

Notes

Notes

Date		Score
	_____vs_____	

Match

Date		Score
	_____vs_____	

Match

Date_____

Date		Score
	_____vs_____	

Match

Date_____

Date		Score
	_____vs_____	

Tips for coaches

1. In soccer the result should never be the first priority. Your objective is to develop the talents of young players.

2. Does this mean that you cannot make any demands on your players? Of course not! You can require them to perform well, but not to achieve a given result. Try to win on the basis of positive soccer ideas and the skills of the individuals on the team, but not on the basis of putting the result first. Make it clear to your players that if they earn seven out of ten for their performance when they could have had an eight, then they have performed below par. In this case criticism is justified.

3. A good way of looking at performance in this way is to give (written) evaluations at fixed times. At the same time you can agree new objectives to be achieved before the next evaluation. Let the players make their own evaluations, and in this way make it clear to them that the progress of each individual player is more important than the team's position in the league table.

4. Players must play at the highest possible level commensurate with their physical and mental attributes and their talent. A coach is on the wrong path if he stops a player from moving up to the next level during the season on the grounds that, for example, this will weaken the coach's team and spoil its chances of winning the league.

5. Players develop quickly at a young age. They should therefore be given the opportunity of playing in lots of positions on the team. A more definitive choice of a player's best position should not be made before the age of 14 or 15.

6. In principle the best players should be given an attacking role. This will enable them to develop their creativity more quickly in tight situations in the face of greater resistance. Attackers can always be converted to defenders at a later stage, but making attackers out of defenders is more difficult.

7. Try to convince the club committee that equipment for players' training sessions should not be the last item in the budget. It deserves top priority. Pay attention to the weight of the ball used for training sessions.

8. Aim to give individual coaching to goalkeepers and the most gifted players.

Ruud Gullit:

"With talented young soccer players you have to pay attention primarily to technique and insight. Tactical insight is evident even at a young age. For example when a player makes a certain pass at exactly the right moment. Technique can always be improved, but you have to be born with tactical insight. It is extremely difficult to learn."

individual qualities of the players. Be sure to take account of the characteristics that typify young players at various ages, and to apply general training principles.

By evaluating the session afterwards you will be in a position later to make use of past experiences or solutions.

11. Reach firm agreements concerning:
  • match preparation
  • warming up
  • non-attendance
  • studying in relation to playing soccer
  • treatment of injuries

12. Varied training sessions are not necessarily the best training sessions. Repetition is important.

13. Be enthusiastic. Do not seek excuses for failure. Keep abreast of developments in the world of soccer.

9. Make sure that no one can put one over on you. Always ensure that you can prove your case to players, parents and committee members by keeping an exact record of match details, attendance at training sessions, reserve players, analyses, etc. In short: make good use of this soccer companion.

10. Plan the training sessions properly. The coaching objectives should be match-oriented and based on the

Communication

As a soccer coach you will sometimes also have to fulfill the role of counselor. Good communication with the team and the individual players is of great importance. A lot of information is either not communicated, or is changed and distorted in the telling. This is really the basic problem of communication. Communication can be greatly improved if coaches and instructors are alert to, and attempt to avoid, some of the causes of poor communications.

Key reasons for poor communication:

1. Verbal communication is unclear and incomplete; words have their limitations.

Just listen to some of the instructions that coaches shout from the sideline: "anticipate", "look", "make an opening", "go for it", "wake up", "find space." If these shouts are simply intended as encouragement there is no problem. But sometimes a coach really wants to give instructions and get his message across during a match. What are the players to make of the above instructions? Anticipate what? Look where? Make an opening - how? Go for it - how? The coach is not making himself clear. People often use words differently, and some words are inherently vague.

2. Non-verbal communication is distracting and may be misunderstood, or too little attention is paid to it.

Gestures, body language, distance apart and tone of voice impart very important signals. However, we are not always aware of them. Sometimes they transmit information that the sender would rather keep hidden. For example, during a tactical discussion (which is taking too long), players may fidget in their chairs, or do not look at the coach, or whisper to each other.

3. The coach fails to get his message over properly.

Clarity is an important part of communication. A coach may mumble, or be incapable of presenting his message in a logical sequence, or try to impart too much information, or fail to check whether he has been understood.

4. The coach fails to listen properly.

For example if the coach fails to concentrate, or has his mind on something else (so that he listens with his ears but does not look at that player and therefore misses an important piece of information) or has some preconception, then everything is seen in a different light.

5. "Noise" during the transmission of information.

"Noise" is an external distraction. This can result in large blocks of information being missed.

Feedback

Information must be transmitted properly, because it is certain that if something is capable of being misunderstood, then it will be.

What should you do if you have even the slightest doubt about whether information has been transmitted correctly? Check it of course! By means of feedback, i.e. by asking questions or asking for feedback.

Asking questions:
• A general question: "Are there any questions about what I have been saying?"
• A specific question: "Is the team formation clear?"
• Checking: "Ron, can you tell me who will take the free kick?"

An important principle is that a coach should keep his talks as short as possible and ask for feedback as soon as possible.

Finally a few tips. Try:
• to inform: Talk when you have the players attention, keep it short, don't try to impart too much information at once, talk clearly and calmly, check that you have been understood.
• to instruct: Focus on essentials, step by step, check that you have been understood, no longer than 1 minute.
• to motivate: Explain "why", refer back to other situations, be enthusiastic.
• to correct: Be positive, focus on one point, show appreciation.
• to stimulate: Use words of encouragement, participate.

Youth Plan Must Be Short and to the Point

Many clubs produce impressive books containing fine objectives, organizational structures, job descriptions, etc. But how all this is to be achieved in practice is often unclear. A youth plan must therefore be short and to the point. Above all it must serve as a basis and a guideline.

If a soccer club wants to draw up a youth plan, the coaching committee should first discuss the various theories of coaching and supervising youth players. It should also discuss the levels at which it wants its representative teams to play. Not too high, but certainly not too low. Players learn more in a category in which they have to fight for points than by becoming champions almost without effort. The number of representative teams a club fields is strongly dependent on the number of talented youth members it has. Qualified coaches are also needed.

The main purpose of a club's representative teams is not to win matches but to promote the instruction and development of talented players. The selection criteria for these teams might be application, technical and tactical insight, attendance at training sessions and motivation. Players in a representative team are not substituted in turn; attendance at training sessions is obligatory; and preparation for a match is more serious. A selection policy should not be applied before players reach the age of 12 to 14. A youth plan can also define:

- selection criteria
- scouting methods
- acquisition and training of coaches/instructors
- the tasks of a youth coach within the youth plan
- core coaching objectives at different ages
- composition of the teams
- coaching facilities and material

So how should we organize things in your opin-

Playing system

The playing system adopted by the club's representative teams can be included in the youth plan. Imagine that the first team plays a 4-4-2 system. The youth plan might then specify that each team will play with only 2 strikers, supported by lots of attacking players who push up from midfield and defense, with plenty of positional switches, overlaps, etc. It might be specified that opponents should be put under pressure as early as possible, so that the team plays as much as possible in the opposition's half of the pitch; that midfielders and defenders should defend positionally; that attacks should be built up by means of combinations; etc.

This guideline can then be translated into a concrete coaching plan with practice drills that are suited to the given objectives.

Coaching

A chapter might be included that deals with general aspects of how to approach training sessions:
There is only limited time available, so only soccer-related exercises and drills should be used.
Vary the coaching routines but remember that repetition is essential. Talk to young players on their own level.
Lots of participation in practice drills, lots of ball contacts.
Lots of small sided games.
Lots of attacks on full-size goals.
Create an atmosphere of enjoyment.
Be critical and dare to make demands, but always be positive.
Give practical examples and coach continuously.

Rules of behavior

A youth plan can also include basic rules of behavior.

Understanding of the role of the referee; referees usually make less mistakes during a match than players.

How do you give the captain clearly described tasks and enough room to carry them out?

How do you promote self-confidence and self-reliance?

Describe the influence of the substitutes' bench and of parents. If the influence is negative, what can the coach do?

How do you intervene when the atmosphere in which the game is being played threatens to take a turn for the worse?

Tasks of a coach

The example below explains how the tasks of a coach can be defined in a youth plan.

A coach should:

• support the policy of the club and translate it into practice;
• be able to make a worthwhile contribution to the team's performance and to the enjoyment of the individual players;
• promote sporting behavior;
• consult with other coaches and participate in monthly coaching discussions;
• be able not only to observe matches but also to coach players with a critical eye;
• be able to conduct methodical training sessions;
• be able to stimulate players and speak their language.

So much for the youth plan. However, a youth plan is only worthwhile if it is translated meaningfully in daily practice and if the club is behind it. The youth plan can be a fixed item for meetings, to ensure that playing soccer will be discussed.

Suggested rules for players

1. Each player must arrive punctually for training sessions and matches. Players must arrive one hour before kick-off for home games, and at the specified time for away games.

2. Each player must attend training sessions regularly.

3. If no transport is provided for an away game, each player must ensure that he has a reliable means of transport.

4. Each player must ensure that his uniform is in good condition and that his soccer shoes are properly cared for. The uniform must include: ....

5. All players must conduct themselves properly with respect to teammates, opponents, referees, managers, coaches and spectators.

6. Wear sports clothing during training sessions and matches. No items of clothing should be worn that are also worn before or after the session or match.

7. Do not wear your normal underwear during training sessions or matches (sports briefs are best, or otherwise a pair of swimming trunks, provided they are not too tight). Take off bracelets, watches and other objects that could endanger others and yourself.

8. Do not eat a big meal before a training session. A light meal is adequate (e.g. a few sandwiches, pasta, milk and fruit).

9. After a training session do not go home alone, especially if it is dark (this applies especially to the youngest players).

10. Do not wear knee or elbow bandages. These should only be worn if absolutely essential, on a doctor's advice. It is however advisable to wear elastic bandages, both during training sessions and matches; they can prevent injuries, provide more support, and give the players more confidence during play and when shooting. Wear shin-pads.

11. Take good care of your sports gear (especially your soccer shoes). If the cleats are of the screw-in variety it is advisable to have two sets: short, rubber studs for hard, dry pitches and long, aluminum ones for soft pitches.
Soccer shoes should always be cleaned after use, and your uniform should always be washed. Get your soccer bag ready on Friday evening so that you won't forget anything on Saturday. Remember that you, yourself, have to play, not your father or mother, so you are responsible for ensuring that you have everything. If you find that you have forgotten something when it is too late, you might even be unable to play.

12. A soccer bag should contain: shirt, shorts, sports briefs or swimming trunks, 2 pairs of socks, tape for your socks, soccer shoes with sufficiently long laces, soap, towel and flip-flops.

13. Socks must be worn pulled-up during the match. Tie a strip of gauze bandage around them. This is better than adhesive tape. Wear your shirt inside your shorts.

14. With regard to selection for the club's representative teams the following applies: players who train twice weekly should be selected before those who only train once or not at all. This rule is subject to the discretion of the coach.

15. If Saturday games are postponed, the coach may decide to organize a training session instead. The players must attend such sessions. Failure to attend can result in suspension or substitution.

16. Performance is the main consideration with respect to the club's representative teams.

If 1 or 2 players are substituted during a match, this is done for specific reasons.

If a given player regularly starts as a substitute or is substituted during matches, the player, coach and manager can discuss whether the player would benefit from a switch to another team. In this way youngsters who would otherwise not get enough playing experience can be helped to play more often. This rule can also be made applicable to the club's recreational teams.

17. The members of recreational teams are treated equally in terms of playing time. The coaches should keep a record.

18. Problems should first be discussed with the coach and only then - if necessary - with the coordinator of your age group.

Rewarding and punishing players

Enthusiastic coaches are always aiming for improvement. Unfortunately, in daily practice this positive attitude often results in constant criticism of players. Too often a coach will focus on faults rather than strengths. This is also true during matches. Many coaches maintain a sort of running commentary on the play, in which they are especially quick to point out players' mistakes: "Terrible pass", "Could you not pass the ball faster?", etc. As a result players often become disappointed, uncertain of themselves or dissatisfied. Anticipatory coaching is much more important and effective than reactive coaching: "Take care, John, you are in the wrong position", "Hold back first, then take up position", "Goalkeeper, don't stay glued to your line". But to do this you have to be able to take a step back from your emotions and the result of the match.

Rewards

Rewarding players is very important, but this should go further than a Coke after the match. The emphasis should be on rewarding the individual during the soccer situation: a pat on the shoulder, praise for a player who gives an assist or makes a good run, etc. Players must feel that they can make mistakes, provided the intention is good. At all times try to ensure that frustration at a poor result is not taken out on others.

However, although rewards are more important than criticism, punishments are sometimes unavoidable.

Punishments

A few tips:

Try to make the punishment fit the crime.

For example: two boys knock the dirt off their soccer shoes in the changing room instead of using the grid and brush provided outside for this purpose. Have them sweep the changing room when the others have gone home.

If player A intentionally kicks player B's ball away during a training session, let player A fetch the ball back.

Ensure that the degree of punishment is in reasonable relationship to the offense committed. Do not allow your irritation to cause you to hand out a heavy punishment for a minor infringement. Even when you are angry, try to remain in control of yourself, otherwise the remedy is worse than the disease. A firm reprimand often suffices to correct a player's conduct.

Intervene as soon as possible after an incident of misbehavior. Do not wait too long with a reprimand or punishment, because that reduces the effect. The ideal to aim for is that unacceptable behavior results in an unpleasant consequence.

Consequences

Besides handing out punishment, point out the consequences of the player's offense. For example, if player A does not pass to player B, player B may decide to stop running into position to receive a pass. If players can be given an insight into the consequences of their conduct, this can serve as a corrective, and help them improve their understanding of the game. Players are frequently unaware of the consequences of their actions. This is an important educational task for coaches.

Fixed punishments can be specified for certain offenses. For example: unexcused absence at a training session can mean relegation to substitute status for half the next match, or arguing with the referee can be punished by substitution. The advantage of fixed punishments is that each player knows where he is and each player is treated equally.

Progressing through the age levels

Clubs invest a lot of effort in bringing on their young players. Nothing can be more frustrating than to see these youngsters then turn their backs on the game. And yet statistics show that this happens on a large scale. The step from youth to senior soccer plays a key role here, alongside a number of social factors such as the enormous choice of leisure activities now available.

Talented players complain at the uncertainty of gaining a regular place in the first or second eleven. They find it hard to assess their own level. Often they are not used to having to fight for their position during their period of youth soccer.

Players who are only interested in playing for enjoyment are put off by the competitive attitude of many other players, and are worried that they will not be taken seriously.

How can a club tackle this problem?

It is important that the switch from junior to senior level is made gradually, so that young players know what to expect and therefore feel more secure. It is important for young players to be involved with the senior elevens during their final season(s). The 'mentor system' can be a good way of doing this. Experienced players with coaching skills can be approached to work with a group of young players, even to the extent that you ask an experienced striker from the first eleven to

Romario

"Modern scouts also look primarily at the physical attributes of a player. You must have strong muscles and be at least 6 feet tall. Each week I try to show that you do not have to be big and strong if you are clever. That enables you to survive at the top too. I became a top soccer player in order to win and to score goals. Even if it is in the final second of the game."

Frank Rijkaard

"If a coach asks eleven players what they want, he will get eleven different answers. A coach must know what he wants from a team and where each individual should play. And if he is not satisfied with a player in a given position, he must approach that player and discuss things with him. Person to person. He must leave the other players out of it as far as possible."

accompany the striker of the team of 12-14 year olds during training sessions and/or before and after a match.

Another good move is to create a J.V. team. This includes:

- the best 14 -15 year olds;
- the youngest players from the first and second teams;
- the reserves from these two teams.

This team can then play matches during the week (e.g. on Mondays) against other J.V. teams or suitable elevens.

In the case of less talented players you can ensure that they remain together during the initial period with the seniors, in the company of older players who can appreciate their situation. It is important that a number of fixed rules from the youth period continue to apply, e.g. the approach to training, non-attendance, secondary activities, preparation for matches, and treatment of injuries.

Clubs that take this approach to the problems of the step from youth to senior level will soon note that their own talented youth players develop much faster than other senior players.

Guidelines for training sessions

1. Avoid long-winded explanations.
   Be short and to the point!
2. Prepare what you are going to say about: organization, drills, movements and/or conduct.
3. Avoid breaking up the flow of your explanation with ums, ahs, ers, etc.
4. Speak clearly, so that everyone can hear you.
5. Look regularly at the group and the individual players as you speak. Does everyone seem to have understood you?
6. Vary the tone of your speech. Change the tempo and pitch. Inject some enthusiasm.
7. Use gestures and mimes to underline what you say.
8. Give the players a chance to ask questions.
9. Repeat the essentials of what you have been saying.
10. Illustrate your instructions with simple examples. Start by demonstrating, then underline this with your explanation.
11. Make sure the players are all relaxed before you start instructing them.
12. Check whether your message is coming over by asking players to repeat what you have said.
13. Restrict the amount of information as far as possible.
14. Do not simply tell players what to do but also why.
15. Monitor whether your instructions are followed, and take corrective steps if this is not the case.
16. Intervene immediately if you detect organizational or tactical errors.
17. Use an instruction board to illustrate tactical situations.

Checklist for training sessions

A training session should conform to the following guidelines. Each session can be evaluated on the basis of this checklist.

1. Match-oriented

- Score goals and try to avoid conceding goals
- Build-up play with the objective of creating scoring chances
- Collective play (win or lose, you are all in it together)
- Direct play/playing to win
- Rapid transition when possession changes

2. Lots of repetition

- Exercise should be repeated frequently
- No long waiting times
- Good planning and organization
- Sufficient balls and equipment
- No long lines

3. Adjustment to the group

- Take account of the players' age group
- Take account of their skills
- Take account of their enjoyment

4. Proper coaching

- Explain what the team is trying to achieve
- Let the players learn for themselves
- Demonstrate what you want
- Give instructions
- Suggest solutions

6-10 year-olds

Learning through playing

Characteristics

For children of this age, the starting point is being able to play soccer spontaneously and enjoyably with friends of the same age. Everything is strange and novel. The process of getting used to rules, equipment, pitch, accommodation and guidance is central. In general there is little sign of competitiveness or the urge to achieve. Children have a playful approach and are largely concerned with themselves, with their own movement and runs as well as their concentration on the ball. This egocentric approach means that tactics and combination play take a back seat. The child's first aim is to win the ball and the second is to run after it. The result is usually a disorderly tangle of bodies around the ball. It is totally against a child's natural instincts to run away from the ball (run into space). Children are excitable, mobile and easily distracted at this age, and they are strongly focused on their coach.

Leadership

As a coach, try to maintain an air of calm and friendliness at all times, no matter how unconcentrated the children appear.

Try to experience things through their eyes, to enter into their world.

Punish a child rarely if ever! Reward for doing something well is often much more effective than punishment for mistakes.

Maintain contact with parents. Parents are a valuable source of information about a child's behavior.

Marco van Basten
"When I score a goal I experience an 'oceanic' feeling of joy; joy that comes from the very depths. It is not the same when someone else scores, no matter how good a goal it is."

Coaching tips

Start the training session with a game, either with or without a ball (warming up). If more than one coach is present, form smaller groups. Keep the games and exercises simple. If children are asked to do something which is too difficult or complex this can have a negative impact on their motivation. Learning through play should be the motto. The emphasis should be on all types of small-sided games and positional games. Games of 4 v 4, 5 v 5 and 6 v 6 on small pitches with alternating goalkeepers should be a central feature of training sessions. The goals should not be too small, so that lots of goals can be scored. The aim of playing soccer is to score goals, so this should be a central element of training sessions. Getting the players used to the ball, the rules, the playing area and the resistance of the opposing players are the most important coaching objectives at this age. The coach should restrict himself to the bare theoretical outlines of the game, e.g. the team in possession must try to score, the team without the ball must try to prevent the opposition from scoring and try to regain the ball as soon as possible. Instructions should be simple, e.g. 'Try to win the ball back as quickly as possible', 'Don't just wait for the ball', 'Don't stand still'.

Summary: Ensure that everyone is active; small groups; one ball per player; no long lines; brief explanations based on demonstration; lots of variation; lots of praise. Show that soccer is a fun game.

10-12 year-olds

Learning by playing

Characteristics

This is the ideal age for acquiring and honing motor skills. There are a number of reasons for this. The youngsters' physical development is harmonious, and control of the body is therefore good. At this age children are capable of learning new movements very quickly, they are not frightened of experimenting and their physical coordination is excellent. They want to be grown up, and they compare themselves to their contemporaries. Competitiveness and the urge to achieve increase. They have no fear because they have not yet learned to think about the consequences of their actions. At this age children start to become less self-centered and more group-oriented. Group values, standards and rules apply. The group formulates its own rules and laws. Children have to learn to win their own place in the group and to build contacts.

Leadership

Maintain good contact with the players. This is a two-sided process. Speak to the players in their own language. Reward good performances. Children of this age like to

---

Johan Cruyff

"In modern soccer, strikers have very little space. It is therefore important for young players to be taught at an early age what they should do in scoring positions. Hitting the ball first time is one of the hardest elements of soccer. Even during training sessions you must control the ball quickly and shoot, whether or not there is an opponent nearby. You must retain this concentration and attitude even after you have already scored a few goals during the training session or match. Scoring goals must become a habit."

Wiel Coerver teaching soccer fundamentals to young players.

be praised. Rewards often achieve more than punishment. In this phase children develop a strong sense of justice, with regard to the rules of behavior as well as the rules of play. Make sure that the rules are clear, and monitor them consistently.

Challenge the youngsters occasionally. If done light-heartedly this is more effective than always being serious. 10-12 year-olds want to achieve, and a coach must be able to put results and achievements in the right perspective from time to time.

Coaching tips

This is a good age for learning movement techniques. Demonstration is of great importance. During practice, check that the movement is carried out properly. Motivate players by explaining why certain movements have to be carried out just so. Positional games and small-sided games form the basic coaching tools. Tactical aspects such as running into space and taking up position, hanging back, playing one-twos, creating space, switching the direction of play and direct play are dealt with, as are aspects of technique such as passing, shooting, dribbling, running with the ball, controlling the ball and going past an opponent. Another important objective is learning to play together as a team. The organization of the team and of the different lines within the team are central to this phase. However, the coach should never lose sight of the fact that the enjoyment of playing and movement are the main priority.

Summary: Children have a great capacity for learning at this age, and the basis of their soccer achievements must be formed during this phase. Give them the chance to achieve, and work consistently towards forming a team.

12-16 year-olds

Approaching the match

Characteristics
Physical growth accelerates during this phase. Differences in rates of growth, and differences in the age of onset of accelerated growth, lead to wide variations in performance. Physical control and coordination often suffer. Sometimes one player will be judged as being better than another when in fact he is simply going through a period of more rapid physical development. The players' physical development is accompanied by radical changes in their mental development. They become more aware of themselves as individuals and become more critical. This can result in conflicts, stubbornness and hot-headedness. Players at this age place considerable importance on social contact with their contemporaries, especially in a group context.

Instruction
It is often almost impossible to teach players anything when they are going through a negative phase. They are easily distracted, hypersensitive and lacking in coordination, and this may seem to indicate a loss of motivation for soccer. Try to retain a positive attitude. During puberty players may be overanxious that they might fail. Of course, this varies from player to player. Find out how far you can go. The desire for independence and responsibility means that players frequently want to express their opinions and be listened to. Let them have their say on various topics. Let them ask questions. The way the coach handles himself sets an example for his charges.

Coaching tips
Instruction in technique is extremely important. If a movement is learned badly, it will be difficult to change it later. The players' tactical development can advance rapidly in this phase. This means that the team becomes a unit, and players are confident enough to engage in a dialog with each other and give each other instructions. Positional games are a very important part of the process of tactical instruction. Do not assign exercises to develop strength; this can cause injuries and may distort balanced growth. The ability to perform for longer periods increases.

Summary: Soccer must be enjoyable during this phase, because the players are unsure of themselves. Be patient and ensure that the players are not asked to do too much. Show understanding of individual shortcomings and problems, and do not make too many demands.

16-18 year-olds

Performing well in the match

Characteristics
The players' become appreciably stronger and faster. The biggest changes are on the psychological and social level. Becoming an adult means daring to accept responsibility and being able to cope with responsibility. There is an increasing need to play a role in decision-making processes.

Instruction
Team talks about tactical matters are worthwhile at this age. Make sure the players know that they can always discuss things with you. Instruction can be kept brief if the players are already familiar with the content. Encourage the players to correct each other.

Coaching tips
During training sessions, teach the players to become used to giving each other instructions. Specific conditioning exercises can improve players' technique. On the pitch the players' fulfill specific roles. This means that they have responsibilities. Tactical tasks must be within a player's mental, physical and technical capabilities. It is probably advisable to let the best and the oldest youth players participate in senior training sessions during their final junior year.

Summary: At this age it is possible to focus on team performance. Specific conditioning exercises with the ball are worthwhile, as are team discussions.

Warming up

Warming up before a training session

Warm-up routines may vary in accordance with the objectives of the training session.

Acceleration and sprint training require a different type of warming up to a session of technical and tactical coaching.

Bearing this in mind, it is still possible to ensure that warm-ups are sufficiently varied. The coach must always remember that he is dealing with soccer players, and he should therefore use a ball as much as possible. He should also try to make the warm-up enjoyable. This can be achieved by introducing lots of variation into exercises and small-sided games.

This is an important part of coaching. Players should first warm up individually (short runs with the ball, stretching). The players must exhibit self-discipline and accept responsibility themselves. The coach can play a monitoring role. After this individual preparation the coach can switch to collective warming up.

What are the optional and obligatory elements of a warm-up?
- Running to relax the muscles
- Stretching exercises

- Suppleness exercises
  - alone
  - in groups of two
  - with/without a ball
  - running exercises
  - cross-field passes
  - short passes
  - jumping
  - knee lifts
- Exercises requiring
  - strength and skill
  - individual
  - groups
  - with/without equipment (ball)
  - with/without resistance
- Technical/tactical exercises
  - with a ball
  - individual
  - groups of two or more
- Small-sided games
- Games of tag

The coach must plan each warm-up and decide which elements should be emphasized, taking into account factors such as the weather, the objectives of the training session, the mood of the group, etc.

Warming up before a match

As already mentioned, warming up is largely a matter for the individual. And before a match every player's mind will certainly be focused first and foremost on preparing himself for the game.

Each player must use his experience of the various exercises to decide how long and intensely he needs to warm up. This means that some players will go out onto the pitch before others.

Warming up can last for 20 to 30 minutes.

A warm-up before a match may include:

- Gentle running
- Stretching exercises
- Running exercises
  2 or 3 increases in intensity;
  Between these increases,
  relaxed running and suppleness
  exercises alternating with 6 to 8
  short sprints.
- Warming up with a ball
  This can be based on each
  player's position:
  wingers cross the ball
  strikers and midfielders shoot
  at goal

Heading

Passing and moving in two groups of five (possibly with a specific set-up, e.g. 3 forwards + 2 attacking midfielders, or 4 defenders + 1 defensive midfielder) taking up positions to receive the ball

- large area, small areas
- 2-touch, 1-touch play
- positional game (3v2)

After the individual physical preparation and specific work with the ball, two groups of 5 can be formed.

Two sessions of 2 to 3 minutes in a small area. 1-touch play. Take up position and after each pass accelerate/sprint (concentration).

Alternate this with long passes along the ground and through the air (low intensity).

Brief period of relaxed running.

Stretching exercises

Stretching the muscles of the shoulder girdle, torso and hips

Exercise 1 (see Photo 1):
Hold the left wrist with the right hand and count to four while gradually bending diagonally to the right, forwards and sideways.

Photo 2:

Photo 1:

Exercise 2 (see Photo 2):
Stretch as far as possible to the side with both hands behind the neck, so that the right elbow points down and the left elbow up. Hold this position for at least ten seconds, because the muscle needs at least ten seconds to attain its greatest length. The main muscles that are stretched in this way are the latissimus dorsi and the triceps.

Stretching the muscles at the front of the thigh

Exercise 3:
Take the right foot in both hands and tilt the pelvis backwards by tightening the muscles of the abdomen and buttocks. The knee of this leg should point diagonally forward. Pull the foot higher against the lower back to increase the tension. This stretches the large femoral muscle (quadriceps femoris).

Photo 4

Exercise 4 (see Photo 4):
Lie on the left side and pull the right foot towards the right buttock. The right degree of stretch of the front muscle of the thigh is achieved when the heel is just not touching the buttock.

Stretching the muscles at the back of the thigh and the lower leg

Exercise 5 (see Photo 5):
To stretch the calf muscle, move one foot about half a yard backwards; both feet should point straight forward and the heel of the back foot should remain on the ground. Keep the back leg stretched and bend the front leg. The body should lean forward in a line with the back leg in order to increase the tension in the calf muscle. This exercise stretches the calf muscle (gastrocnemius) that runs behind the knee and is attached to the bottom of the femur.

Exercise 6 (see Photo 6):
Now bend the back leg and shift your weight to this leg. Push the right knee down to the ground. This stretches the Achilles' tendon and the calf muscle (soleus).

Photo 5

Photo 6

Exercise 7 (see Photo 7):

Lie on your back and move the knee of your bent right leg as close to you as possible. Now take hold of the back of the right lower leg and stretch the leg, pulling it towards your face.

Photo 7

Photo 8

Stretching the muscles on the inside of the thigh

Exercise 8 (see Photo 8):

Stand with your legs stretched apart, feet pointing outwards. Bend the left leg but keep your weight in the middle. Support yourself with your hands on the ground. Count four until the muscles in the right leg begin to hurt. Use your left elbow to push the left knee as far back as possible. Hold this position while you count to eight. Try not to let the left knee come past the left ankle, and do not let both knees point inward. To achieve this, pull the toes of your right foot towards you. Switch after counting to four and bend the right knee.

Exercise 9 (see Photo 9):
Sit down, lean forward, and press both elbows against the insides of your knees. Hold your ankles while doing this (not your toes!). Hold this position while you count to eight, then relax while you count to four. Do this exercise, and all other stretching exercises, two or three times.

Photo 9

Photo 10

Stretching the muscles of the back and neck

Exercise 10 (see Photo 10):
Lie with your back on the ground and pull your knees towards you, trying to touch them with your nose. You will feel your back and neck stretching. You can also pull just one knee towards you.

Stretching the muscles in the lower back

Exercise 11 (see Photo 11)
Make a round back, tighten the abdominal muscles and push the middle and lower back upwards and backwards.

Photo 11

Photo 12

Stretching the muscles on the outside of the right thigh and the back

Exercise 12 (see Photo 12):
Cross the right leg behind the left leg. Both legs can be slightly bent. Turn the upper body to the left, so that you can reach the right heel with both hands. Remain in this position while you count to eight. Repeat on the left side.

Preparation

Start of the season

A coach must be able to plan well in order to prepare his players for a new season. A coach who leaves it to the club secretary to arrange practice matches may suddenly be confronted with opponents who are much too strong, with all the physical and mental consequences for his team (injuries, etc.). A coach who fails to take account of his players' vacation periods may have to start with an unbalanced selection, in which false expectations may play a role.

The following list should help you to be well prepared to start the important initial period.

1. Start of the season

When will the first official league or cup match be played? Deduct the number of training sessions you require, and you then have the date of the first training session of the new season.

2. Vacation

As mentioned above, it is important to have an overview of the players' vacation plans at an early stage (June/July). You can then see whether you will have to give some of the players homework, and whether you will be forced to compress the preparation period.

3. Number of players

Especially in the world of youth soccer, it may be necessary to find out the number of players at the initial training sessions. A group of 30 requires a lot more preparation than a group of 16.

4. Number of training sessions

At least 15 training sessions are needed before a team is ready to play its first match. The structure of the training sessions is dealt with later in this book.

5. Number of matches

For the players, a new coach automatically means that more friendly games have to be played. This is also the case when the group contains a large number of newcomers. It is not unusual to play 5 to 10 practice games. Do not start with the strongest opponents.

6. Training camps

Even for amateur clubs and youth teams, it is worthwhile considering whether to organize a training camp. Such a camp offers an ideal opportunity to build up team spirit for the rest of the season. The rules must be clearly formulated from the very start, otherwise the group will formulate its own rules. During a training camp there is more time to practice restart plays, discuss basic tactics, formulate objectives, etc.

7. Content of training sessions

It is clear that fitness will be important during the initial phase. This topic is dealt with in detail later in this book. In addition you need to develop a playing system that suits the abilities of your players, rather than one based exclusively on your own soccer philosophy. Your tactical coaching can then be based on this system. You can do this best by means of good coaching during small sided games and positional games. During such preparation you also need to coach basic techniques, routine moves and restart plays. After agreements have been reached and practiced, it is better not to treat restart plays in isolation but to repeat them frequently during small sided games.

During the preparation phase, careful warming up and cooling down (ten minutes jogging and stretching) are important in order to avoid injuries and help players to recuperate faster.

Rinus Michels

"I only include players in my team who will try to win, by one means or another, over the whole ninety minutes. This applies to each confrontation, even during a training session or a friendly match. You must make the players realize that they must not let their opponents play. I call this the anti-soccer complex. By whatever means, you must prevent the opposition's play from disrupting your own organization. All means are allowed that the game of soccer offers. I only pick players who are prepared to carry out, without any reservation, their appointed tasks within the context of the team's tactical plan. Only when this has been achieved do you have time for your own game, and then I choose a playing concept with a form of build-up aimed at hitting a long forward pass as soon as possible. Because a long forward pass results in a healthy number of opportunities to score quickly, to exert pressure in the opposition's penalty area, to

create scoring chances for the players moving up from midfield, in short to play spectacular, exciting, soccer."

8. Enthusiasm

It is especially important for a coach to radiate enthusiasm during this period. He can do this best if he has a good physique and is mentally strong. He must be completely refreshed when he approaches the new season and can only communicate pleasure in playing if he is also in condition to participate.

9. Setting objectives

It is important to set realistic objectives for the group as a whole and the individual players. How does the group assess its prospects? What pressures are the club's committee and sponsors exerting? What are the individual expectations? As coach you must always indicate clearly whether expectations are justified. Only one team can win the championship!

Start of the second half of the season

The winter period and the winter break can nowadays be regarded as a second preparation period, corresponding in many ways to the period before the season starts.
During this phase too, the players' conditional build-up must be well balanced.

This is a difficult period for players and coach, because bad weather often makes pitches unplayable. Training sessions also have to be carried out under difficult condi-

tions. Coaches are often expected to demonstrate their creativity in terms of finding suitable facilities for training sessions (this too is a question of early planning) and adapting practice drills to the conditions. The basic principle should be: training sessions must always take place. This period of the season is also a good time to take stock of your progress and ask questions.

- Do we need to amend the objectives we set ourselves at the start of the season (i.e. make them more realistic)?
- Do we need to introduce new routines into our method of play, and how do we go about this in terms of the necessary coaching?
- Should the restart plays be changed?
- Can we integrate any new players into the team in the second half of the season?
- Should we implement any activities to improve the morale of the group?
- Are any individual discussions necessary?
- What does my own future as a coach with this club look like?
- What external influences are there on the group of players, and can I deal with them adequately?
- How can I set up a feasible scouting system with an eye to next season? (It is necessary to

take stock of the current group of players first, including the younger players who will be moving up into the group).

In short: the winter period is a good time for taking stock of your progress and, if necessary, making adjustments in order to ensure that everyone is well prepared for the most important part of the season.

Fitness training

Anyone who coaches must be able to organize his time effectively, because there are only a few hours available for coaching each week. It is therefore not advisable to spend lots of time running through the woods, lapping the pitch or sprinting from post to post. That would be a waste of precious time.

In modern soccer, a responsible coach must choose types of exercises that are closely related to match practice. Of course there are a few basic principles that apply to all fitness training:

- there should be a gradual build-up in terms of the effort required
- there should be lots of variation in the exercises
- there should be a good relation-ship between work and rest periods

These principles can be readily incorporated in positional and small sided games.

Homework

If you can only coach the team for two or three hours each week, the players must realize that they need to work on their conditioning at home. Priority can be given to the important back and abdominal muscle exercises. Players should also warm up independently before a training session, because this also saves precious time. (Naturally you will initially have to supervise the players and check them regularly.)

Leo Beenhakker
"During training sessions I emphasize that the interests of the team come first. Only then can the team function properly and only then can its stars shine. If a star is in form it is like playing with an extra man. But a star must realize that when he is not playing well he still has to perform his tasks within the team as a whole. If he does not do that, you will have days when you seem to be playing with a man short."

Endurance training

Fitness training should start by improving general stamina by means of endurance training. Most technical exercises, such as those of Wiel Coerver, are suitable for this purpose, as are positional and small sided games, provided certain aspects are emphasized:
- play 6 v 6 line soccer on a large pitch (e.g. half of a full-sized pitch)
- only touch the ball a limited number of times (depending on the players' level of skill)

Intensive endurance training

The next phase is intensive endurance training. Suitable exercises include:
- forcing the team in possession to move up quickly (each player must be over a given line before the team can score)
- a fixed sequence of actions

(control the ball from a throw-in, play a 1-2, take the ball to the goal line, cross the ball, make a goal-scoring attempt). Such a sequence allows you to work on the specific conditional elements associated with a given position. For instance, you can let the same player hit all the crosses, or make all the goal-scoring attempts.

Interval training

The next stage is interval training. It is important to realize that moments of intense exertion during a match, such as sprints down the flank by an attacking full back, rarely last more than 30 seconds. It is therefore pointless to make players exert themselves to the limit for periods of 2 or 3 minutes. It is also worth knowing that the recuperation period after a session with lots of interval training is two or three days.

You start with light interval training (heart-rate no higher than 20 to 30 beats below maximum). The period of exertion should be short, but frequently repeated.

This is followed by intensive interval training: heavier exertion, less repeats, but longer relief periods. As a rule of thumb, relief and exertion periods should be equal, i.e. an exercise that lasts 1 minute should be followed by a relief period of 1 minute to allow the player to recover.

Interval training exercises:
- 2v2 as line soccer, with one-on-one marking (5 series of one and a half minutes)
- Dummy in the middle: the players in the middle have to keep chasing after the ball (5 series of 1 minute)
- Circuit training: the full back passes to a midfielder; the winger sprints into the middle, creating space for the advancing full back; the midfielder passes to the full back, who crosses the ball to the winger; the full back then walks back to his original position (5 repeats).

Speed training
You can achieve good results with players in the 10-13 year-old age group with running technique exercises. Subsequently it is difficult to achieve any genuine improvement in speed. Speed training should again be based on the real situation during a match, and this means that distances should be short (5 to 30 yards).

Good exercises are:

- 1v1 with finishing on goal, after which the beaten defender must sprint after the attacker to force him to run faster
- The winger is given a start on the full back at the start of the exercise; the full back must try to prevent the winger from crossing the ball (5 to 10 repeats)

Strength
Shooting, heading and sprinting require explosive strength. Exercises should again be match-related:
- leaping to head a cross
- heading game in a restricted space with two full-size goals
- finishing from various positions after a short sprint

Match
During a match you can also impose additional conditional requirements:
- play a pressing game against a weaker opponent
- play a counter-attacking game against a stronger opponent, with three or four players sprinting forward to follow-up the long forward pass

- play one-touch soccer as much as possible, depending on the situation and level.

Specific conditioning
Exercises for players who have more time for training, or have specific problems, e.g. lack of strength, aggression or agility, can be found in the next chapter.

Specific conditioning

1. Aggression
Objective: to develop positive aggression in players and to channel this properly, so that it is harnessed in the interests of the team.

Groups of two (players A and B): A lies on his back and B prevents him from getting up by holding him against the ground. B then sprints away. A jumps up and sprints after B. The exercise is then repeated.

2. Agility
Soccer players often have to function under pressure in limited space. These exercises teach the feet to do what the brain tells them.

Groups of two (players A and B): A sits with outstretched arms and legs. His legs should be slightly bent so that they are not quite flush with the ground. B skips rapidly over A's arms and legs.

3. Speed
Objective:
1. Speeding up the important initial movement from a variety of starting postures: standing, sitting, lying, etc.
2. Breaking up the monotonous rhythm.

Groups of two (players A and B) play the 'shadow' game: A makes sudden series of varied movements forwards and sideways - jumping, sitting, hopping, etc. B must imitate these movements as well as he can.

4. Strength - explosive strength

Objective: to improve the strength of the whole body. During pre-season preparation the emphasis will first be on absolute strength, then on speed. This means mainly static exercises during the first phase, then dynamic exercises.

Static exercise for groups of two (players A and B): A lies on his front with his legs bent. B sits behind him and holds A's legs at the back of the heels. A tries to bend his legs up and B presses down on A's heels, giving a resistance to the pressure.

Hans Westerhof

"I will never accept intimidation of a player by other players. Neither during a match nor during training. It may be necessary to shout if a player is not concentrating. But I cannot accept it when players try to cover up their own mistakes or take out their bad temper by picking on someone else. That has a detrimental effect on the victim's game and therefore on the whole team. My players know that they will then be substituted immediately."

5. Speed of reaction
Objective: to react to situations faster and better.
Ensure:
- good level of tension in the muscles
- powerful natural reflex
- well balanced sequence of movements

Two players (A and B) stand opposite each other. A has his hands behind his back. A stretches his arm sideways to shoulder height and B kicks upwards to touch the A's outstretched hand.

6. Coordination exercises

Objective: to teach a player to make lots of different sport-related movements in the shortest possible time so that his movements become faster and more efficient.

Groups of two (players A and B): A crouches on his hands and knees. B lies on his back to A's right. B jumps up, jumps over A, and then lies on his front to A's left. B repeats the exercise, then A etc.

7. Flexibility and suppleness

Extending muscle sensation while retaining muscle strength. Wide patterns of movement so that all the muscles of the body can be felt. This considerably reduces the risk of injuries, and these exercises have a conditioning effect on the various groups of muscles.

Extent of movement:

- 100% or slightly less: hold this position while counting to between 6 and 10
- 70-80%: slowly wave in patterns of movement
- 50%: feel all your muscles briefly, prepare for the next movements

Exercises to develop strength
(groups of 2, with and without a ball)

1. From a press-up position, one player catches the ball as it is thrown by the other player and throws it back: vary left, right, low, high.

Arm, shoulder girdle and back muscles are used in this exercise.

2. One player lies on his back (with the other holding down his shoulders), raises his out-stretched legs just off the ground and moves them through a circle. For abdominal muscles. Longitudinal and transverse abdominal muscles.

3. One player lies on his front, raises his upper body to get hold of the ball when the second player rolls it to him, and

throws the ball backwards over his head to the second player. Develops back muscles.

4. Perform press-ups. Hold both legs, hold one leg. Body and legs outstretched. Move forward, backward, sideways. Arm, shoulder girdle and abdominal muscles are used.

5. One player lies on his front, pushes up into the press-up position, then jumps over the second player's leg as the second player rolls to the other side. Arm, Shoulder girdle and torso muscles are used in this exercise.

Exercises for groups of two, one of whom offers resistance

6. Horse and rider
The 'horse' is resisted by the 'rider', who moves right and left and up and down.
  The 'horse' must remain upright and walk in a straight line.
Leg, abdominal and back muscles

7. One player sits with his upper body bent forward. He then tries to move his upper body backwards until he is lying on his back, while the second player tries to stop him. Back and abdominal muscles.

8. One player lies on his front and raises his upper body. He then tries to lower his upper body to the ground again, while the second player tries to stop him. Abdominal muscles.

7/8

TRAINING METHODS

	Endurance method	Interval - extensive
Objective	Improve basic stamina	Improve specific stamina
Intensity	60 - 80%	80 - 90%
Heart Rate	140 - 160	170 - 180
Lactic acid content	+/- 2 mmol	2 - 4
Duration	20 - 80 minutes	3 - 6 minutes
Recuperation	1 - 2 minutes	1 - 3 minutes
Repeats	1 - 5	10 - 20
Exercises	Run through the woods	Positional and small
	Small sided game (6 v 6)	sided games
	Small sided game (8 v 8)	3 v 3
	Small sided game (11 v 11)	4 v 4

	Interval - Intensity	Repetition training
Objective	Improve speed and stamina	Improve speed
Intensity	90 - 100%	100%
Heart rate	Maximum	-
Lactic acid content	4 - 6	-
Duration	1 - 3 minutes	5-40 minutes (+/- 5 repeats)
Recuperation	2 - 6 minutes	2 - 3 minutes
Repeats	5 -10	2 - 5 series
	1 v 1 competition	Shooting practice
	2 v 2 competition	Sprint races
		Sprint and shot

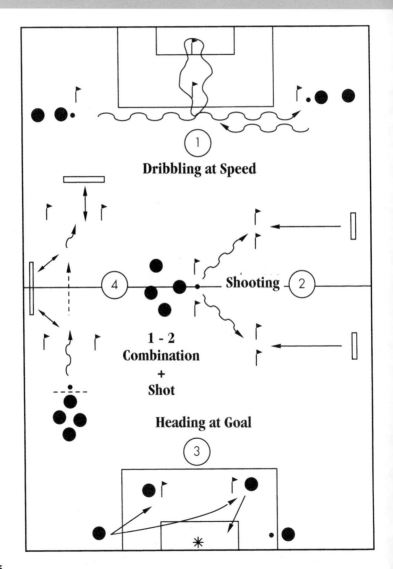

Dribbling at Speed

1

Shooting 2

4

1 - 2 Combination + Shot

Heading at Goal

3

✳

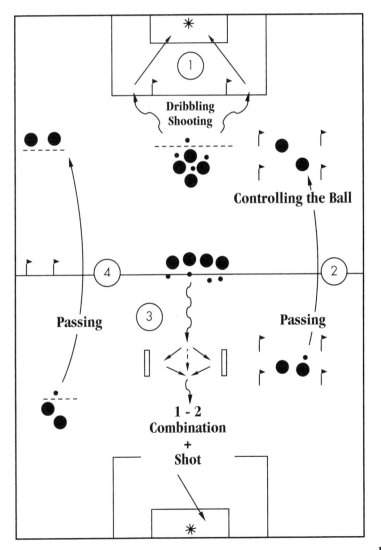

Dribbling
Shooting

Controlling the Ball

Passing

Passing

1 - 2
Combination
+
Shot

146

Positional games

Positional game of 3v1
with 6 players + 2 goalkeepers
- In the attacking half 3 attackers try to score against 1 defender (3v1).
- If a goal is scored or the defender intercepts the ball, the defender quickly crosses the halfway line into the other half, where he and the other two players become the attackers. One of the initial attackers must also run back into this half to play the role as the defender. If the defender intercepts the ball the 3 attackers must try to regain the ball immediately. A goal can only be scored when all the attackers are over the halfway line.

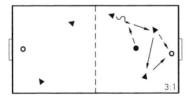

Points to note
- pitch not too large (15x30)
- switch quickly
- how to attack so that defense cannot be suddenly exposed
- sometimes patience is needed
- possible limitations

Positional game of 3v1
with 8 players + 2 goalkeepers
- In the attacking half 3 attackers try to score against 1 defender (3v1)
- If a goal is scored or the defender intercepts the ball, the ball goes to the other half, where another group of 4 plays 3v1.

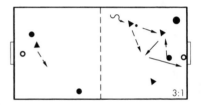

- In contrast to the game described above, no players have to move from one half to the other.
- It is important that the 3 attackers who are not in action take up positions that will allow them to attack quickly and effectively when they are given possession. (They should not all stand on the halfway line.) The defender must take up the best possible tactical position.

Positional game of 3v2

with 6 players + 2 goalkeepers

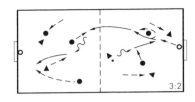

- In a 3 v 2 positional game the attackers' numerical advantage is smaller and it is therefore harder to attack.

Individual runs and overlaps can feature more.

If the attackers lose possession, four of the five players must join the one player in the other half, where 3 attackers again try to score against 2 defenders. This game is very intensive, with frequent changes of possession and switches from one half to the other.

Positional game of 3v2

with 8 players + 2 goalkeepers

- In a 3 v 2 positional game with

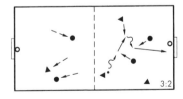

8 players, the defenders can play 3 v 2 in the build-up if they win the ball.
- From 3 v 2 in the build-up to 3 v 2 in attack.

Positional game of 3 v 2

with 10 players + 2 goalkeepers

- In a 3 v 2 positional game with 10 players, none of the players has to switch from one half to the other.
- It is important that the players who are not in action remain tactically alert and take up good positions.

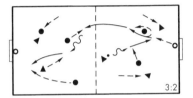

Positional game of 4 v 2

in which all 6 players switch halves

- The 4 attackers try to string together 10 passes without the opposition intercepting the ball.
- After the 10th pass the players all switch to the other half and again try to string 10 passes together.
- This is repeated until, for example, 5 mistakes have been made, at which point 2 other players take over the defending role.
- Which group of 4 switches most often from the one half to the other?
- Possibly introduce restrictions.

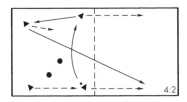

Positional game of 4v2

with 8 players in 4 groups of 2, and switching from one half to the other

- This 4v2 is played with 4 groups of 2 players.
- 4 attackers play against 2 defenders in one half, while the remaining group of 2 is in the other half.
- When one player in each of the 2 groups of 2 making up the 4 attackers has touched the ball, the ball can be passed to the group of 2 in the other half.
- The player who makes the pass and his colleague, together with the 2 defenders, move into the other half.
- If the ball is intercepted the 2 defenders become attackers.
- The attacker who gave the ball away and his colleague become defenders.

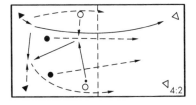

- How often can the attackers switch from the one half to the other?

The positional game is played as a small sided game with the halfway line as a limitation for the defending team. One or more players of the defending team may not enter their own half, so that the attackers have a numeric advantage over the halfway line.

Positional game of 4v2

with 8 players + 2 goalkeepers

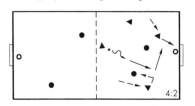

In contrast to the 3v1 positional game, more players are involved in the attacking and defending play. The attackers have to create more chances. The defenders must communicate with each other. When the ball is intercepted more players (4) must switch halves quickly and be tactically alert.

Here too restrictions can be introduced or tasks assigned, e.g. 4v2 in the build-up in the team's own half, switching to 4v2 in the attacking half.

Positional game of 4v2

with 10 players (2 goalkeepers)

In a positional game of 4v2 with 10 players, it is important for the players who are not in action to remain alert and attentive. They must take up position so that, when they are given possession, they can attack quickly and effectively.

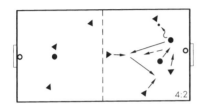

Positional game of 4v3

with 12 players + 2 goalkeepers

- In a game of 4v3 with 12 players, more than half of a full team is involved
- Some aredirectly involved around the ball and the player in possession
- Those involved indirectly, take up positions (players who are not directly involved in the play)
- Numerous technical aspects can be dealt with.
- The coach can intervene at various tactical moments.

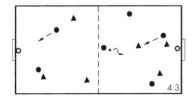

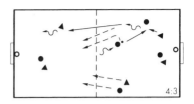

Positional game of 4v3

with 10 players + 2 goalkeepers

- The number of players involved in the positional game is larger.
- Attacking play requires more thought.
- Tempo changes, etc. Defenders must communicate well: when to mark man-to-man, when to mark zonally, when to double team, when to challenge for the ball, etc.

Positional game of 6v3

within the penalty area

- Played with 9 players (3 groups of 3) inside the penalty area.
- 6 players try to keep possession as long as possible.
- If the 3 defenders intercept the ball they try to score in the full-size goal.
- Restrictions can be introduced, e.g. players in the group of 6 must touch the ball 3 times.

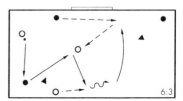

Positional game 3v3

with 12 players + 2 defenders, and switches of position

In the positional game of 3v3 the objective is to use switches of position as a means of surprising the 3 defenders.

One player from the team in possession can push up into the attacking half. One of the attackers must fall back to his own half, so that a 3v3 situation is maintained in each half.

This game results in lots of changes of position and opens up more chances for the attackers. The defenders must switch faster and organize better. The emphasis can be placed on the changes of position and takeover of tasks.

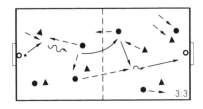

3:3

Goalkeeper's warming up before a match

How should a goalkeeper warm up? The goalkeeper is the first member of his team to go onto the pitch, about 35 minutes before the match starts, followed immediately by the reserve goalkeeper. Together they start to warm up by trotting from side to side of the pitch while playing the ball to each other. The exercises then follow in increasing tempo.

1. Standing with legs apart, holding a ball, the goalkeeper stretches, lifts his arms, then touches the ball to the ground between his feet. Repeat 5 times.

2. Standing with legs apart, holding the ball, the goalkeeper sways with the ball from left to right and vice versa. This is repeated 10 times.

3. Standing with legs apart, holding the ball, the goalkeeper stretches alternately to the left and right. This is repeated 5 times.

4. First with his legs slightly apart, then with his ankles crossed, and his body bent forward, the goalkeeper makes short pushing movements with the ball in front of his body.

5. The goalkeeper then trots to the center of the goal. The reserve goalkeeper kicks a few balls into his hands from a distance of about 10 yards - along the ground and at waist and chest height.

6. The reserve goalkeeper then hits a number of gentle shots from different positions in the semi-circle on the edge of the penalty area.

7. These exercises with the ball are now interrupted by a physical exercise without the ball: standing with legs apart, the goalkeeper bends forward and moves his shoulders and arms in a circle.

8. The reserve goalkeeper shoots at goal from the edge of the penalty area, first from directly in front of the goal, then from right and left.

9. The reserve goalkeeper hits 5 lobs towards the goalkeeper from 30 yards in front of goal. The goalkeeper catches the ball and returns it by alternately kicking and throwing.

10. The reserve goalkeeper hits 3 crosses from the right corner flag.

11. Now the reserve goalkeeper hits crosses from the touch-line, 20 yards from the goal line (repeat 3 times), followed by 2 long forward balls from the halfway line, 3 crosses from the left and again from the corner flag.

12. 10 hard shots to right and left of the goalkeeper from the corner of the penalty area.

13. Hard shots from about 15 yards, so that the goalkeeper has to dive.

14. A final series near the goal, with the reserve goalkeeper shooting at the goalkeeper from close in (reaction).

15. Various pace shots from the forwards from different angles.

"A goalkeeper must be a powerful jumper. This determines whether you can reach the ball, and get up high enough above your opponent so that he cannot interfere with your arms."
(Pim Doesburg)

Goalkeeper coaching

Game forms

In this book we devote attention to an important element of goalkeeper coaching: game forms in which, under pressure and often with a lot of enjoyment, the basic techniques are tested.

Game form 1:

One goalkeeper in goal, two goal-keepers near or behind the goal to fetch the balls, and two goalkeepers 15 yards out. The latter try to score as many goals as possible in a peri-od of 1 minute. Balls that go wide or over the goal are immediately fetched back.

After 1 series take a rest for 1 minute and then change position. Competition between the 5 goal-keepers. Who will let in the least goals?

Hans van Breukelen
"A goalkeeper must have more self-confidence after a training session.

He must believe that he has made some fantastic saves."

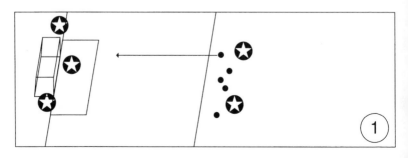

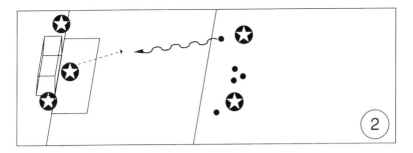

Game form 2:

The same as game form 1, but now the 2 players take turns to move in on the goalkeeper and try to score. Also in competitive form.

Game form 3:

Much can also be learned from a game of 4v1.

Mark off a playing area of 5 x 5 yards with cones.

Four players (goalkeepers) in the corners (not static). The goalkeeper in the middle tries to score as many points as possible by intercepting or touching the ball during a given time and the other players try to prevent this.

Rules of play:

1. Depending on the technique of the players in the corners, they can touch the ball three times, twice or once.

2. The first ball is free and the goalkeeper is not allowed to intercept it.

3. If the goalkeeper manages to get hold of the ball he scores 2 points.

4. If the goalkeeper only manages to touch the ball he scores 1 point.

5. If a player hits the ball out of the playing area, this counts as 1 point for the goalkeeper, who then has to fetch another ball from near the playing area.

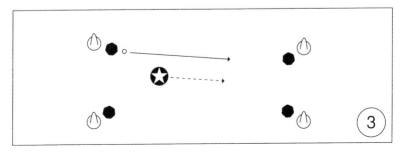

6. If the ball is played between the goalkeeper's legs he forfeits all his points.

Game form 4:
Goalkeeper tennis soccer

Objective of the game:
To volley the ball so that it hits the ground in the opponent's court.

Rules of play:
Goalkeeper A serves by volleying from the back of the court. Player B must return it. If player B catches the ball he can volley it back into A's court from the place where he caught it (He cannot take more than 1 step to volley the ball).

Points:
- If the ball hits the ground in the opponent's court: 2 points
- If the goalkeeper tips or punches the ball outside the court: 1 point
- If the ball passes under the rope or lands outside the opponent's court: 2 points

Serving:
- Serve from the back of the court at the start and after each point. Change of service can be regulated as in volleyball or table tennis.

Variations:
- Serve by drop-kicking the ball rather than volleying it.
- Raise the net (to about 6 feet). No kicking the ball, just throwing.
- Increase or decrease the size of the court.

Game form 5:
Objective of the game:
To score in the other goalkeeper's goal by throwing the ball.

Rules of the game:
Goalkeeper 'A' begins from his goal line. he throws the ball towards goalkeeper 'B's goal. 'B' saves the ball. When he catches the ball he can take a maximum of 2 steps towards 'A' before throwing the ball

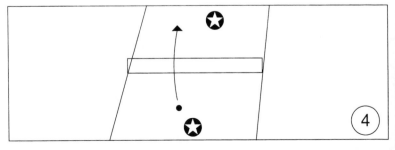

towards A's goal. If a goalkeeper tips or punches the ball out of play, his opponent gains possession. Neither goalkeeper can cross the halfway line.

Points:
- Each goal scores one point.
- Serving/restarting or starting play: always from the goal line at the start, after a goal, or after the ball has been tipped or punched out of play. Change ends after a certain time or after a previously agreed number of goals.

Variations:
The goalkeeper can only:
- throw the ball with a round-arm or bent-arm throw;
- kick the ball from hand;
- volley or drop-kick the ball;
- kick the ball from the ground;
- the defending goalkeeper scores if the ball bounces in front of him.

Make the playing area smaller or larger.

If the goalkeeper shoots or throws the ball wide of the goal or over the bar, his opponent scores a point.

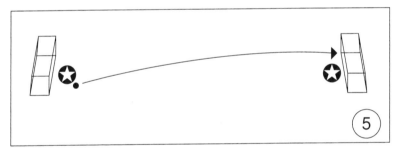

What are tactics?

Whichever system of playing is chosen, the most important basic principle remains: you defend and attack with eleven players. In the case of young players very little organization is needed, for example the right back defends the zone on the right in front of his own goal and the center forward plays close to the opposing goal. Regardless of the tactics, the most important thing is to keep moving in order to find space.

Defending

A defender aims to force the attacker to one flank, reducing his scope for action. It is important to defend the zones, i.e. everyone stays in his own position and picks up the opponent who moves into his zone. If no opponent appears, cover your colleagues. The closer you are to your own goal, the closer the opposition has to be marked. Always take up position between your opponent and the goal and try to prevent him moving inside. The best way to defend is to intercept the ball before your opponent can bring it under control. If possession is lost the whole team must help to defend.

Build-up

One of the most important passes in build-up play is the cross-field pass. Although midfielders often have space to run with the ball, passing is much more effective. Alternate short and long passes.

Attacking

It is easiest to attack down the flanks, because that is where there is the most space. Always try to get behind the defender. Attacking play must be aimed at scoring a goal. The only thing that matters is: how can we get the ball into the goal as quickly as possible? You will often see all the strikers running towards the opposition's goal when a midfielder has the ball. This is a mistake. It is better for one striker to take up an advanced position and for the others to move towards the player in possession. Attackers must frequently switch positions by making runs across the field to try to confuse the defenders.

Learning tactics

Dribbling

The three basic elements of dribbling are: movement, acceleration, speed, and the ability to unbalance an opponent. Never dribble in your own penalty area. Feints and speed are the dribbler's key weapons. Keep the ball close to your feet when you dribble.

Learn to dribble in a varied tempo (slow-fast).

Learn to shield the ball (keep your body between the ball and opponent). Remain observant while dribbling, keeping your head up, so you can see what your opponent does and what your teammates do.

Only dribble when it is necessary (no possibility of passing, creating a scoring chance). Let the ball do the work whenever possible; do not run with the ball if you can avoid it.

Dribble as little as possible in your own defensive zone - if you lose the ball it spells danger for your own goal. While dribbling you must think (what is the best thing to do in this situation?), react (to defenders who try to intercept the ball) and be aggressive (when you go past an opponent).

Feinting and passing technique

Learn to feint by using your whole body or by slowing your run.

Unbalance your opponent (put him on the wrong foot) and then go past him. Accelerate after feinting.

It is easiest to beat a defender by taking the ball past his standing leg (the leg carrying his weight).

As an attacker, keep the ball moving.

Vary your movements.

Do not try to beat a defender in your defensive zone; this is always a big risk.

Passing

Play the ball simply and do not try to make an excessive curve.

If possible, play the ball along the ground.

The player without the ball determines how you play it (to his feet, to run onto).

Alternate long and short balls. Do not telegraph your intentions by constantly looking in the direction in which you intend to play the ball.

Learn to use the cross-field pass. If you have a scoring chance, take the initiative. Do not lay the ball off to someone else because you are frightened of failing. Act at once and do not hesitate. Every second you lose gives the defenders more chance of recovering.

Goalkeepers should learn the drop-kick; this can be directed very accurately.

Receiving a pass

Do not let the ball bounce.
Go towards the ball.
Do not let the ball go past you.
Bring the ball under control as
quickly as possible.

Heading

Timing is the key element of heading, but jumping ability and physical coordination are also important.
Always aim to meet the ball at its
highest point. Attackers should
always try to head the ball down
towards goal. Retain your concentration by keeping your eyes open.

If you make a header on the run
this helps you to jump higher and
get more power behind the header.

Defenders should not wait for a
high ball to bounce but should head
it directly.

If a defender is close behind you,
take a step forward to give yourself
more space.

Try to meet the ball at its highest
point (timing).

Coaching a team

Regardless of the result, preparation for the next match begins directly after the final whistle of the current one. As a coach you have to be able to analyze the shortcomings of your team and the individual players. On the basis of this analysis you draw up the coaching objectives for the following week, taking care not to neglect your long-term planning. If you want to discuss the match with the team, remember that the players who have performed badly may feel very threatened by such a discussion. Face-to-face discussions during training sessions may produce better results. As a coach you certainly should not varnish over mistakes, but you should always beware of robbing players of their self-confidence.

It is advisable to announce the team sufficiently early. Some coaches wait until just before the match kicks off, in order to keep the group on its toes. However, it may be more important to give the selected players the time to concentrate on the task they will have to fulfill during the coming match.

Ensure that the players feel secure. Hans Westerhof, coach of FC Groningen, formulated this as follows: "It is very important that players in a team know where they stand. With that in mind, each play-er in my group knows that he will be picked for one of only two positions. The players know these positions and there is therefore no confusion. No player will be asked to play in left midfield one week, on the right wing a week later, then as sweeper the next week."

Involve the substitutes in the match discussions. Tell them what tasks they might have to take over if they get onto the pitch.

The match itself

Arrange to meet in good time. Remember that you have to set an example. A coach who expects discipline from his players must himself be punctual. Inspect the pitch so that you can, if necessary, give advice on the correct footwear.

Guus Hiddink

"As a coach you have to work not only on the players' physical condition but also on their mental condition. You can do this by stimulating and provoking them. Small sided games are ideal for this. I go to the limits of what is acceptable in these games. Infringements are often tolerated if there is no danger of injury. I deliberately withhold praise from players who need to become mentally stronger. The players are pushed until they gain the necessary maturity. Of course you have to ensure that the players do not go too far and that such a small sided game does not deteriorate into a physical game."

Sometimes it may be necessary to adjust the team's tactics. If the ground is very soft, for example, it is not very wise to try to build up from the back with short passing movements, because this will increase the chance of losing the ball.

Discuss the main points briefly with the team. Insist that all players should be out on the pitch warming up well before the start (about half an hour before kick-off). Be prepared for possible injuries. Observe your team and your opponents during the warming up period, this may provide valuable information. During the match remember that a coach who is constantly shouting at his players has not done his work properly during the preparation for the match. Try to distance yourself from your emotions and analyze the opposition's system of play during the first five minutes. Some adjustments may be necessary, especially if your team does not include many experienced players. Sometimes it may be sufficient to tell a single player to make an adjustment. After this initial stage the coach's field of attention must take in far more than the immediate play. It may be necessary to give instructions to players who are not in the direct vicinity of the ball in order to prevent a problem situation from arising.

Half-time

During the half-time interval the coach must ensure that his players can genuinely relax. Stand in one spot and try - no matter how emotional the game has been - to radiate an air of calm. It should only rarely be necessary to read the riot act. Ask if any of the players need attention, insist that they all sit quietly, then give a short talk. Repeat what was agreed beforehand, and point out what has gone wrong. Summarize what has happened in the first half in defense, build-up and attack (perhaps using one player from each line as an example). Give brief instructions and reassure the players. A practical tip: ensure that the water is within reach (assign this task to the manager). This avoids unnecessary irritation.

In the second half it is often necessary to make substitutions. Letting the substitutes warm up may stimulate the players on the pitch. Give clear instructions to the substitute players in respect of the changes you want to be made on the pitch.

After the match the mood may be ecstatic or funereal. After a win make sure you let the players know that they earned their success. At such moments the players are receptive and you may be able to give a brief analysis of the match. After a defeat things are more difficult; try to remain in control of your emotions, and try not to make the mistake of summing up everything that went wrong and looking for scapegoats. After a defeat you should remain with the team as long as possible. Of course it may sometimes be necessary to show your anger and disappointment - for example, if the team showed a lack of effort - then you can leave the team to think

Jan Reker

"As a coach I am always very calm in the dressing room - also at half-time. It is not my style to shout at the players or throw chairs and tables around. I get the team together and first of all the players get the treatment they need. If they want ice they can have it. Some might need a refreshing drink. I then expect them all to give me their full attention for three minutes. The fixed sequence is then: Is anyone injured, does anyone have any tactical problems? When these points have been dealt with I tell them briefly what tasks are not being carried out as agreed and explain the changes I want to make."

about their performance. After a win it is better to allow the players to be alone. Reach an agreement before the start of the season that individual players' performances will never be discussed negatively.

A youth team coach should avoid getting involved in discussions with parents after a match. Tell the parents that you will be glad to see them after the following training session. Finally: remember not to neglect the substitutes. Shake hands with them, also those who were not used, and thank them for their cooperation. Lose no time in telling the players who were substituted the reason why. This may avoid problems during the next training session.

Restart Plays

The free kick
Free kicks should be rehearsed during training so that each player knows exactly what he has to do. The players must be alert and concentrated. Because each player knows what the others have to do, they can monitor each other on the pitch. This encourages team spirit.

The free kick directly in front of goal
Defenders:
A wall must be formed consisting of about 6 players. The goalkeeper and the player at the end of the wall must ensure that the wall is positioned correctly. Two players must stand near the wall, ready to try to block the shot. The other players cover the strikers and other options.

Attackers:
A number of specialists should take up position around the ball. A scoring attempt can take the form of a hard shot or a swerving ball over or around the wall. If this is not possible another variation can be chosen (not too complicated).

The corner
Defenders:
At least 9 players should fall back into the team's own penalty area. There should be a player on each post, and man-to-man marking in the center with one covering defender.

Attackers:
There are various options (inswinger, outswinger). The players must know who will take the corner, who will move up from defense, etc. Because a corner represents a direct scoring opportunity, the team must be well organized on the edge of the penalty area.

An alert third line positioned near the halfway line must prevent the counter-attack.

When the corner is taken each player must be convinced that the ball will arrive at the right spot, and must be prepared to keep moving and take a gamble. The players must not forget their tasks for an instant.

How to deal with injuries

During preparation for the new season the most frequent injuries are caused by overuse through excessive training. Groin and Achilles' tendon injuries in particular fall into this category. Because the players' general condition after a vacation is often below par, this also applies to torn muscles and muscle strains in the thigh and calf.

Blisters are an everyday problem in July and August, when pitches are often bone hard. How can these sport injuries best be treated, and what can a coach do when a player with such an injury wants to resume training with the group? The answers to these questions are given in this chapter.

Groin strains

This is probably the most common form of injury during the pre-season period. A distinction can be drawn between:
a. The traumatic groin strain:
A strain which occurred during a forceful movement such as a sliding or block tackle.
b. The insidious groin strain
This appears gradually and - especially if it is neglected - becomes steadily more serious. Usually it is caused by a small physical abnormality, e.g. a slight difference in leg lengths, a foot abnormality, a hollow back.

The insidious groin strain is the most difficult to treat. The cause must be eliminated if recovery is to be permanent. The extra use at the start of the season most frequently causes this form of strain to appear.

Therapy

Numerous soccer players who consult their doctor on account of a groin strain are advised that the solution is a period of rest. Rest is certainly necessary during the healing period, but medical science offers a number of techniques to accelerate this process, e.g. shortwave diathermy, electric muscle stimulation, massage or suitable stretching exercises. In the case of insidious groin strains it is essential that treatment is accompanied by action to alleviate the cause; this can vary from posture exercises for players with a hollow back, to correction of foot abnormalities with an insole.
Summary: advise a player with a groin strain to rest and to have the injury treated professionally. Find out whether the strain is traumatic or insidious.

After the healing process

When a player wants to resume training, advise him to build up

gradually:
Start with a run of 20 minutes, not on the road but on grass. The player should listen to the signals from his body. If the pain returns after 15 minutes - however slight it may be - he should stop immediately; his body is telling him that the limit has been reached.

The day after the first run should be a rest day. In the case of many players the pain will return on this day. This is an indication that the exertions of the first day were too great.

If no pain is felt, a longer and more intensive run can be undertaken (35 minutes).

The player can then resume training, but it is not advisable to join in with the group immediately. The player should work alone with a ball - after a good warm-up with specific stretching exercises for the groin. Start with passing and shooting with the instep or the outside of the foot. Use the inside of the foot only in the final stage, because this puts most strain on the groin. Make sure the ball is not too heavy. If there are no after-effects, the player can resume training with the group.

Test

There is a simple but effective test for determining whether a groin strain is properly healed. In the sitting position, place your fist between your knees and then press both knees powerfully against it. If you feel pain in your groin, you are not yet ready to resume training or playing.

Injuries to the Achilles' tendon

The Achilles' tendon is poorly supplied with blood 1 to 2.5 inches above the heel, and this is the place where injuries most often occur.

The nature of such injuries makes them feared. They may recur very quickly.

An Achilles' tendon injury often begins with only slight discomfort. If you ignore this, in the course of time you can compare the tendon with a rope that starts to fray. Such a tendon may then suddenly tear.

Therapy

During the initial stage a 20-minute massage with a piece of ice, repeated 3 times each day, can be very effective. A practical tip: use a piece of ice shaped like an popsicle, and rub it along the inflamed tendon.

If the problem persists, complete rest is necessary, together with active medical treatment. Consult a doctor. Just as with a groin strain, the cause of the problem must be identified. This may be a foot abnormality, shortened calf muscles, or a serious ankle injury suffered at some stage in the past. After such an injury the Achilles' tendon functions differently and is very susceptible to overload. During the injury period it is often possible to ride a bicycle perfectly well, and this can keep the condition reasonably in check.

After the healing process
After the Achilles' tendon has healed the player must exercise strict self-discipline, because such injuries tend to recur very quickly. Running must be approached more carefully than after a groin strain. A soft surface is essential, as are good, stable jogging shoes. This injury frequently affects joggers who run on roads! If no discomfort is experienced during the initial runs, a simple test can be carried out to indicate whether the player can resume training with the group.

Test
Stand on the leg with the healed Achilles' tendon. Stand initially with the foot flat against the ground, then lift it slowly until you are standing on your toes. If you can do this without experiencing discomfort or pain, then the healing process is very advanced or even complete.

Nevertheless, caution is advisable when the player returns to the soccer pitch. Explosive exercises such as sprinting, jumping, sudden changes of direction and turning should be avoided at first.

Torn muscles and muscle strains
In soccer players these occur mainly in the thigh (front and back) and calf.

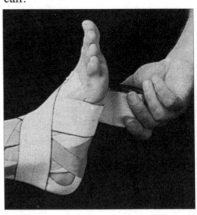

Therapy
The first treatment after the injury occurs is of crucial importance. If an injury is not given the right treatment immediately, the recovery period can last as long as 8 weeks instead of only 2.

A frequently encountered - and very important - acronym in this context is RICE: rest the injured leg (R), apply ice (I), apply compression (C) and elevate the injured leg above heart level (E).

This regime should apply for the first 24 to 36 hours, then the injured player should consult a (sports) doctor or physiotherapist.

The next phase is very important. If the injury is treated properly the player feels almost no discomfort from the injury, and many players are inclined to resume full training and start playing again. There is then a considerable risk of suffering a new strain or muscle tear. Wearing a bandage during a match does not help at this early stage, although it can provide some support during light running exercises.

The strain causes a scar in the muscle, and this must become strong enough to withstand renewed stress. During normal everyday life this does not take long, but in a match situation the stress on a muscle is 10 times as great and a scar is not yet up to this after only a few weeks. The golden rule for these injuries is therefore: be especially careful for at least 2 weeks after you think the injury is fully healed. Do not participate in pressure exercises or matches during this period.

Test

Perform the familiar stretching exercises for thigh muscles and calf muscles to determine whether you feel any discomfort. Then stretch the relevant group of muscles to the maximum. If you have no problems the first time you do this after suffering the injury, this marks the start of the final two extra careful weeks.

Blisters

Finally we turn to the treatment of blisters. Bursting them accelerates the recovery process, provided it is done hygienically and the blister is then treated immediately with iodine. A band-aid should then be applied, otherwise there is a considerable risk of infection.

To conclude we would like to emphasize that injuries in pre-season require self-discipline from both player and coach during the recovery process, together with rest and professional treatment, and that the player should take great care when he resumes training and playing.

Medical supervision of soccer players

Prevention

For soccer players, too, it is true that prevention is better than cure. It is therefore of special importance that:

- physical complaints that arise during training or after a match are immediately reported
- close attention is paid to food and clothing
- players get enough sleep

Over-training

Growth (and young soccer players are clearly in a phase of growth) is often accompanied by complaints such as headaches, back pains and pains in the joints. Although these complaints are certainly painful they give no cause for worry. With lots of rest and a reduction in training they will soon disappear. However, it is important to report these symptoms, because they coincide with complaints resulting from the so-called over-training syndrome.

Symptoms of over-training are:

- poor performance on the soccer field
- loss of appetite or reduced appetite
- sleeplessness
- poor results at school
- irritability
- sudden loss of weight
- high pulse rate
- dizziness
- attacks of excessive perspiration
- dissatisfaction with everyone and everything, especially the coach, who is blamed for the player's poor performances

The only remedy for over-training is a reduction in the amount of training the player does. Mental stress (e.g. during the school examination period) and infectious illnesses can also cause the above symptoms.

Feet

Young soccer players who work hard and take a healthy approach to their soccer development must ensure not only that they keep both feet on the ground, metaphorically as well as literally, but also that their feet are in perfect order. He can do this:

- by washing them, and above all drying them, thoroughly after matches and training sessions
- by cutting his toe nails properly (not too short)
- by checking the soles of his feet regularly for blisters, infections or athlete's foot
- by treating small cuts or breaks in the skin between the toes in order to prevent infection (such infections can cause groin com

Dick Advocaat

"I get very annoyed when I see small goals used for small sided games during training sessions for young players. Usually there is also a goalkeeper in a goal no more than 1 yard wide. Why do we not use goals a few yards wide? That encourages the players to score as many goals as possible. Young players get more enjoyment out of winning 7-5 than 2-1."

plaints, because the lymph nodes in the groin react to them)

- by never going barefoot in washrooms and dressing rooms but always wearing shower slippers
- by reporting foot complaints immediately. They may result from an increase in weight and height. Changes to training exercises may cause such complaints to disappear. If complaints are not reported in time, a player may have to take a period of complete rest.

Clothing

Just as the feet are by far the most important parts of the body, footwear is the most important item of clothing. A player's soccer shoes must be cared for properly. Regular cleaning is just the beginning. soccer shoes should never be allowed to dry in front of a source of heat but should be filled with newspaper and allowed to dry naturally. Soccer shoes with screw-in cleats should never be used during training sessions or matches on a bone hard ground, because the cleats press too strongly into the soft sole of the foot. Screw-in cleats are best suited to soft ground (4 x 0.5-inch cleats at the front and 2 x 0.6-inch cleats at the back). Check the insole and heel of the soccer shoes to ensure that there are no rough areas. The climate varies widely with the seasons, and clothing should be worn to suit the prevailing weather. In winter a warm tracksuit cannot be regarded as a superfluous luxury. Jewelry, such as chains, rings, armbands, earrings and buttons is not permitted during training.

Food

As the amount of work performed during training increases, so does the appetite. Instead of eating more, it is better to change your eating habits so that you eat smaller amounts but more often. Eating a full meal before a training session or a match should be discouraged. A rest period of 2 to 2.5 hours between eating and training or playing is advisable. Eat fresh vegetables and fruit rather than fatty food.

Lifestyle

As the amount of work performed during training increases, it becomes important to incorporate sufficient rest periods into the pattern of life. Especially after training or a match, rest is of crucial importance. Going out with friends can also be a form of relaxation. On the other hand smoking is a very questionable activity and is disastrous for building up and maintaining good physical condition. Those who have not yet started to smoke are best advised not to do so. And those who have started would do better to stop.

Sef Vergoossen

"When I am dealing with players, my method of analyzing a match with the group is not dependent on the result. I try to make it clear that soccer means more than being able to kick a ball around. If a team is leading 2-0 but not playing well I might criticize the players in no uncertain terms during the half-time break. And if a team is leading 6-0, the game should never end 7-1. Players must appreciate that they cannot relax if they are stronger than their opponents. They must learn to give their best, 90 minutes long. Players who understand that will become something special, because they will have the inspiration to go to the limit."

Tips for attracting new club members

In the context of attracting new members it is important to realize that just a single activity will not yield much in the way of results. A whole cycle of activities must be organized to ensure that a larger number of new members can be signed up for a longer period. The starting point could be, for example, a soccer open-day. Invite a famous professional soccer player or coach, show a short but spectacular soccer video, and make sure there are plenty of activities in which the visitors can participate themselves. Ensure that there is a relaxed atmosphere, and make parents and accompanying adults welcome. A lot of work has to be carried out before such an event is held, e.g. it must be ensured that it is well publicized.

Tips:
Advertise in local free press rather than regular newspapers.

Adapt your use of language to your target group. Ensure that your copy is delivered before the closing date. Personal invitations, e.g. via schools, are even better. Involve the club's own players (it is a good idea to organize a soccer workshop at a local school).

Such an event must be followed up by other activities to ensure that potential new members are repeatedly confronted by the club within a short period of time:

- via a follow-up to the publications around the open-day
- by invitations to participate in training sessions
- by playing practice games with the new members

Our future is in the hands of

First-aid

1. Ensure that qualified first-aid helpers are present at all your club's sports activities.
2. Assign one person to carry out weekly checks on first-aid boxes and replenish them when necessary.
3. Ensure that the first-aid box is always kept in the same place and that it is accessible to the first-aid helpers (i.e. preferably not behind lock and key).
4. If the first-aid box is in a locked room, ensure that a key is available during sports activities.
5. Always indicate clearly where the first-aid box is kept.
6. Ensure that there is an accessible telephone with a list of important telephone numbers, e.g. doctors, ambulance service, hospital, etc.
7. Ensure that the gates to the sports terrain are open or can be opened during sports activities to give access to an ambulance if necessary.
8. Assign someone to meet the ambulance at the gate and guide it to the site of the accident.
9. Place notices clearly indicating that it is forbidden to park in front of the gates.

Public relations

A club needs a good public relations policy to ensure good contact between the members themselves and between the club and the public. The club uses PR to raise its profile and to foster understanding of what it is doing. It is important that everyone in the club is in agreement about the image the club should project.

There are various groups who must be kept informed:

- members
- future members
- public opinion (neighbors, newspaper readers)
- influencers (parents, schools)
- sources of subsidies (town council, sports council)

Each group must be informed in a suitable manner. It is important to work to a plan as much as possible, and for the committee to be in agreement on the message the club wants to put over. There are many conceivable ways of putting over a message, e.g. a well designed club guide at the start of the season. This is important for the youth section in particular, and such a guide is a good visiting card for new members.

A club guide can contain information such as:

- important addresses and telephone numbers
- procedures for joining the club
- descriptions of how to get to the grounds of less familiar opponents
- rules for the youth section
- the teams fielded by the club
- short history of the club
- information about uniforms

Other publications are conceivable, e.g.:

- a club magazine or newsletter with fixed topics
- reports about the club in a local newspaper
- an article in the newspaper once each season
- a well maintained information board (update the information promptly, in a legible form, with attractive layout, and not positioned too high - the youngest members must also be able to read it)

PR can also be of importance in letting club helpers know that their work is appreciated: a cup of coffee for youth coaches or parents who provide transport, or a small gift at the end of the season or at New Year (e.g. flowers for the partners of the youth coaches).

Fund-raising

A club needs a lot of money to provide adequate facilities, uniforms and activities for its members. Ideas for raising money are therefore always welcome.

Many clubs make the mistake of

Now and then they received a gift of a ball but naturally this did not help very much. It was decided to mount a campaign to remedy this situation, but without forgetting the two-way aspect. Shopkeepers were approached to contribute enough money for a ball, and in return a number of small balls were hung in

concentrating solely on the money provided by the various contributors and forget that this should be part of a two-way process. Sponsors have their own interests and this should be recognized. A sponsor is some-one who gives something and who receives something in return (pub-licity, better image, more sales). An example: a club had too few balls and other training equipment.

a net in the club's facilities, with cards attached showing the name of the sponsor, an advertisement with the shop's logos was placed in a local free newspaper, and the sponsors were invited to attend the following youth tournament, where they were received with coffee and cakes. This campaign was so successful that sponsors sponta-neously offered help in other areas (e.g. uniforms).

The familiar sponsored run can also raise a lot of additional money. The club members seek sponsors who will reward them for their efforts, usually involving completing a number of rounds of a course, with or without obstacles. The money raised from the sponsors is donated to the club. Youth members in particular are very keen to raise a lot of money in this way. (NB: agree on a maximum number of laps, otherwise the sponsors may find themselves having to pay more than they bargained for.)

It is important to involve large sponsors in such an event. Organize a VIP run during such a sponsored run, so that sponsors can participate and hand over their contributions in person. The two-way principle also applies here. Ensure that everyone receives a small souvenir, and hang a few special prizes at the clubs facilities (e.g. a shirt with the autograph of a famous player) for players who show outstanding effort or initiative.

Other examples of fund-raising activities are:
- flea market
- sale of articles such as pens, mugs, etc.
- sale of food, e.g. pancake breakfast, baked goods, etc.
- club hats, calendars with a club team photo for each month
- car-wash day

- McDonald's activities: McDonald's offers a number of activities for clubs, and these can raise a lot of money
- donors' campaign
- raffle
- garage sale/flea market

Finally two key points to remember:
- define the sponsor's contribution and what the club will do in return
- conform to the rules of your soccer association

Organizing a tournament

Almost every club committee dreams of organizing a youth tournament. The preparation of such an event takes a lot of time, and it is therefore worthwhile, especially for larger tournaments, to set up an independent tournament committee.

Date

The date can make the difference between the success and failure of a tournament. Anyone who wants to hold such an event at Easter should realize that tournaments are taking place everywhere on that weekend. It may be more sensible to choose a date during the preseason period.

Target group

The committee must often make decisions on such basic matters as: age groups, boys' and girls' divisions. For the club's representative teams or for its recreational teams?

Form

A tournament can take a number of forms:

A. Internal tournaments

1. Club tournament with mixed teams: e.g. teams made up of players from the youngest groups together with one or two older players (perhaps those who plan to become youth coaches).
2. Father and son tournament
3. Tournament with teams of older youth players, teams made up from the coaching staff, teams of parents, sponsors, committee members, etc.
4. A reunion tournament with teams from previous years. This is a good way of involving ex-members in the club again.

B. Tournaments with external participation:

5. Club tournament. Identify local clubs with roughly the same number of youth teams. A tournament can then be organized at various places by swapping teams. Financial aspects can be agreed, a joint program book produced, etc.
6. A championship tournament: in cooperation with the umbrella organization, a tournament can be organized between the champions in a certain age category. In this case the participants may not all be known until a late stage.
7. A tournament for the club's recreational teams, usually the youngest players.
8. A town tournament. Invite various towns to send a team and couple the towns' names

to the tournament.

9. A mini-soccer tournament using the rules of indoor soccer.
10. A 4v4 tournament for the very youngest players.
11. A street soccer tournament on a large square or in a street.
12. An indoor soccer tournament.

The tournament committee

This can include parents, supporters and coaches. Tasks are distributed so that the pressure is not always on the same people.

The Committee

The committee consists of the:
- chairman
- secretary
- treasurer
- coordinator of the sponsors group
- coordinator of the PR group,
- coordinator of the technical group
- coordinator of the volunteers

The coordinators are in charge of the organization of their work groups.

Job descriptions

The following job descriptions can serve as check-lists for the tournament:

Chairman:

- General leadership, chairs meetings
- Monitoring the implementation of decisions
- Contact between executive group and committee
- Representative tasks on the day of the tournament
- Organization of the prize presentation

Secretary:

- Draw up timetable of meetings and agenda, take minutes
- Deal with mail concerning the tournament
- Obtain approval of local authority, soccer authorities, owner of field, etc.
- Formulate, duplicate and mail invitations.
- Contact/by telephone participants
- Process applications to participate
- Draw up schedule of matches
- Draw up schedule for referees
- Draw up rules
- Send confirmations of participation
- Program book
- On the day of the tournament: applications, checking passes, coordinating match results and scores, match documents and disciplinary reports, representative tasks

Treasurer:

- Draw up the budget, and monitor and adjust it during the preparation stage
- Make payments within the agreed period
- Coordinate entrance payments, sponsors' contributions, payments for advertisements, concessions and sales booth takings, secondary activities, etc.
- Collect entry fees on the day of the tournament:
- Representative tasks

Coordinator of the PR group:

- Final editing of the program book
- Designing, ordering and providing posters, invitations, etc.
- Write articles for local press, television information service, regional radio, etc.
- Tape advertising messages
- Provide appropriate music and sound equipment
- On the day of the tournament: man the loudspeaker system, record match results, scores, etc.

Coordinator of the sponsor group

- Discussions with sponsors
- Provision of prizes
- Collect advertisements for the program book
- Proposals for secondary activities during the tournament
- Punctually forward the sponsors' contributions to the treasurer
- On the day of the tournament: representative tasks connected with sponsors and advertisers
- Putting together a sponsorship package

Especially at larger tournaments, which are well known in the region, a sponsorship package can generate more money. The idea behind such a package is that a sponsor can choose from various options. For example:

Package A: $400

- match ball
- advertisement board (to be supplied by the sponsor)
- advertisement in program book (full page)
- advertising slogan on sound system (5 times)
- advertiser's name in local free press or club magazine
- coupling of advertiser's name with well known participant in tournament
- advertiser's name on poster

Package B: $200

- match ball
- advertisement in program book (half page)
- advertising slogan on sound system (3 times)
- advertiser's name in editorial article

Package C: $100

- advertisement in program book (quarter page)
- advertising slogan on sound system (3 times)

Make an attractive folder, in which these options are listed, together with information about the tournament and the club. Hand the folders over personally to the sponsors.

Coordinator of the technical group:

- Sign posting for entrance, parking, changing rooms,

first-aid post, etc.
- Boards for results, standings, food, candy, beverages, sales booths, refreshments
- Extra coat-hangers, decorations such as flags, lamps
- Brighten up the accommodation where necessary
- Looking after the pitches; setting up a tent if necessary
- Setting up the sound system or intercom (field radios)
- Equipment for secondary activities
- Clean-up squad
- Storing or returning items.

Coordinator of other helpers:
- Staff of concession stand and sales booths
- Supervision of secondary activities
- Parking area attendants, supervisors
- Team guides
- Referees' guides
- Back-up team for club workers, teams, guests, sponsors
- First-aid team
- Caretaker

Budget
Finally a few items that may appear on the budget of a tournament.
Possible incoming are:
- contribution per team
- meals
- concession stand (make sure all arrangements are clearly under-stood beforehand)
- advertisements in the program book
- sponsors' contributions
- advertising boards
- income from secondary activities
- subsidies
- entrance money
- parking fees

Possible outgoing are:
- administration and mail costs
- print work (posters, program books, entrance tickets, food and drinks coupons, etc.)
- rented materials (flags, benches, portable toilets , secondary activities, sound system, etc.)
- licenses
- purchase of food and drink, candy, etc.
- looking after participants
- first-aid
- referees
- prizes
- small gifts
- costs of meetings, food and drink for club workers
- exceptional expenses

Organizing secondary activities

You can also make a basic choice between the club's representative and recreational teams in the context of secondary activities. If the representative players get most attention during the season, it is a good thing to give the other players more attention with regard to secondary activities.

A committee can organize lots of different activities for the players, but a good alternative is to provide a basic sum per team to organize morale-boosting activities. Agree a cut-off date for submitting suggestions; experience has shown that otherwise nothing may come of the whole idea and the money will be spent on an end-of-season party, whereas it would often be more useful to spend it during the season.

Many teams save a small sum each week towards an enjoyable afternoon or evening.

Look mainly for soccer-related secondary activities for the club's representative teams, e.g. a visit to a professional soccer match (it may be possible to obtain a discount).

Organize a visit to a local professional club. This might consist of observing the first team training,

followed by a guided tour of the stadium.

For the older players: visit a professional match and make an analysis of the players.

Organize penalty shoot-outs during the half-time break in the first eleven's (U.18) games.

Ask professional clubs to provide demonstration training sessions.

For the recreational teams it is often more interesting to look less at soccer performance than activities which are purely concerned with relaxation.
The possibilities include:
• a table tennis tournament
• a bingo evening
• games
Set out a circuit consisting of about 10 stations. Each team must get round the circuit. Up to 160 players from 10 teams can participate. Naturally the circuit can contain fewer stations. A throw with a large dice determines how many stations you can advance. You have to carry out any tasks you encounter on your way (passing through a gate, heading at goal, line soccer, taking penalties, dribbling, scoring, etc., but also hopping, running in a sack, counting peas, photo quiz, skipping, slow cycling, etc).

- a hexathlon

This can consist of: dribbling and change-of-clothing relay race, a hopping race, a ball slalom in which the players have to clamp the ball between them while they cover the course, an obstacle race and a mummy race, in which one player has to be completely wrapped in rolls of toilet paper - leave gaps so that he can breathe - before his team guides him through obstacles to the other side.

- **attempting to beat the record**

The approach can again be competitive or recreational. Suitable soccer forms are: juggling, shooting at goal, taking penalties, shoot-outs, completing a circuit.

Other record-breaking activities are possible, e.g.: standing crates, boxes or cards on top of each other, lifting as many balls as possible with groups of three, throwing a medicine ball, relay races, water race.

Battle of the stars

A battle of the stars can be an excellent activity for competitive teams. Organize a number of activities during one day, with the ultimate winner being named Sportsman of the year of his team or category.

An example of such a program could be (15-20 participants):

10:00 •	Warming-up
10:30 •	Skills course on the soccer pitch
11:30 •	50 yards swim in swimming pool, then free swimming
1:00 •	Lunch and break
2:15 •	Cross-country cycling
3:15 •	Break, possibly small games
4:00 •	2 mile cross-country run
5:00 •	Presentation of the prizes

Several teams can also take part in this program. The different events then circulate.

Such an activity can considerably improve team spirit, especially in the preseason period (once the players are relatively fit).

Games with fun soccer-type exercises

During the season all sorts of opportunities arise for enjoyable activities outside a playing and coaching context, e.g. anniversary celebrations and tournaments. At tournaments in particular the players may soon become bored during the matches, and a coach often has trouble keeping his charges under control for the whole (long) day. They may get up to mischief, and unsupervised changing rooms may be damaged. Sufficient secondary activities can prevent this sort of trouble and provide a lot of enjoyment.

As an example we describe a number of stations making up a circuit that the players can complete individually or as a team. The number of attempts (3 to 5) depends on the time available and the players' level of skill.

1. Placing the ball
From a line, place the ball accurately into zones marked with points.

2. Shuffleball
With the help of planks make a sort of large shuffleboard and again place the ball accurately from a given line.

3. Shooting dice
A large foam-rubber dice is placed on a cone. Each player shoots at the dice from a line. The number of points given on the dice when it is knocked off is the players score.

4. Target shooting at goal
Divide the goal into zones with tape. Assign a number of points to each zone.

5. Knocking down the cones
Ten cones stand at various heights on boxes. A player must try to knock down as many cones as possible by chipping the ball at them 5 times.

6. Stacking the cones
A player kicks the ball as high as possible out of his hands. Before the ball touches the ground again he must build as high a stack of cones as possible.

7. Soccer golf
A course is set up with the help of small arches. Try to play the ball through the arches. If you fail try again (the ball cannot be played again until it is stationary).
Each player starts with a maximum number of points and loses one point for each failed attempt.

8. The throw-in
Try to throw the ball in so that it bounces in one of a number of hoops placed some distance away. Each success scores one point.

Preseason Training

Objective	Week 1	Week 2
Tuesday	• Comprehensive running, suppleness and stretching exercises • Cooper test - 6 minutes or 12 minutes depending on age • Circuit training with lay-ing off, strength and skill exercises • Small sided games (3v3, 4v4) at fast tempo (2 touch-es)	• running and suppleness • small sided games (4v2); strength and skill • circuit training on basis of intensive endurance training (2v2, 3v1, cross and finish, 1v1) • small sided games with 4 goals
Thursday	• running, positional game (5v2) • circuit training on basis of interval duration (basic technique and strength and skill) • combination games • small sided games (6v6, 4v4)	• running and suppleness small sided games (laying off) strength and skill with accent on heading • circuit training • 2v1 with finishing • small sided games with accent on defense
Saturday/Sunday	• match	• match

Week 3	Week 4	Week 5
• running and suppleness • intensive interval training • finishing after pass to strikers, crosses, play in front of goal • small sided games (3v3, 4v4) or match	• running and suppleness • placing the ball, shooting (groups of 3) • intensive interval training • small sided games (4v4) with full-size goals and goalkeepers or match	• match
• running and suppleness • 1v1 competition • small sided games (2v2) (line soccer) • finishing from lay-off or crosses • attack and defense	• running and suppleness positional game (2v2) with lay-off players • speed training by means of combination plays down the flank • small sided games, attack and defense • tactical talk	• running and suppleness 1-2 combination with groups of 4 • 2v2 with extra man (line soccer) • speed training with play in front of goal • small sided games attack and defense
• match	• match	• match

Preseason Training

Objective	Week 1	Week 2
Technical	• improve feel for the ball by means of basic techniques	• improve basic techniques with emphasis on lay-off, 1-2, or long ball • techniques under pressure
Tactical	• marking/finding space/switching from being in possession to not being in possession in positional games and small sided games	• improve positional play in defense (man-to-man, zonal, covering) • creating 2v1 situations
Conditioning	• improve aerobic endurance • improve staying power • improve suppleness	• improve suppleness • improve staying power • improve aerobic and anaerobic endurance
Mental	• lots of variety training with enjoyment • work on positive attitude and team spirit	• training with pleasure • work on team spirit • uncompromising defense

Week 3	Week 4	Week 5
• improve basic techniques with emphasis on lay-off or long ball	• improve short and long passing	• techniques under pressure
• improve positional play in defense • switching from being in possession to not being in possession	• improve defensive aspects (especially covering - not in a line) • improve play in front of goal	• rapid switch when possession is lost • practice restart plays
• improve explosive strength • improve anaerobic endurance	• improve speed • improve anaerobic endurance	• tapering off - no heavy anaerobic training • speed training
• learning to perform well under pressure (persevere - win your place in the team)	• impart self-confidence	• performing well; increase the pressure

Suggested Coaching Reference Material

Videos

The Dutch Soccer School: Part 1: 40 Offensive Drills for Attacking Soccer
The Dutch Soccer School: Part 2: Attacking From the Back
The Dutch Soccer School: Part 3: Defending
Coaching The Italian 4:4:2 *with Arrigo Sacchi*
Brazilian Soccer Skills and Tactics *with Zico*
German Skills and Small Sided Games *with Otto Baric*
Training Soccer Champions *with Anson Dorrance*
The Soccer Goalkeeper *with Frans Hoek*
Small Sided Games for Functional Training (Italian)
Conditioning for Soccer
Soccer Fundamentals *with Wiel Coerver*

Books

Dutch Soccer Drills: Part 1: Individual Skills
Dutch Soccer Drills: Part 2: Combinational Play and Small Sided Games
Team Building *by Henny Kormelink*
Coaching Youth Soccer the Dutch Way *by Henny Kormelink*
The Manual of Soccer Coaching *by Roy Rees*
Coaching Soccer: Ages 5-12 *by Andy Caruso*
Soccer's Dynamic Short Sided Games *by Andy Caruso*
The Complete Handbook of Conditioning for Soccer

**These books and videos and many others are available from
REEDSWAIN SOCCER BOOKS and VIDEOS.
To order or to get a free catalog call 1-800-331-5191.**